SpringerBriefs in Cybersecurity

T0172004

Editor-in-Chief

Sandro Gaycken, Digital Society Institute, European School of Management and Technology (ESMT), Stuttgart, Baden-Württemberg, Germany

Series editors

Sylvia Kierkegaard, International Association of IT Lawyers, Highfield, Southampton, UK
John Mallery, Computer Science and Artificial Intelligence, Massachusetts Institute of Technology, Cambridge, MA, USA
Steven J. Murdoch, University College London, London, UK
Kenneth Geers, Taras Shevchenko University, Kyiv, Kievs'ka, Ukraine
Michael Kasper, Department of Cyber-Physical Systems Security, Fraunhofer Institute SIT, Darmstadt, Hessen, Germany

Cybersecurity is a difficult and complex field. The technical, political and legal questions surrounding it are complicated, often stretching a spectrum of diverse technologies, varying legal bodies, different political ideas and responsibilities. Cybersecurity is intrinsically interdisciplinary, and most activities in one field immediately affect the others. Technologies and techniques, strategies and tactics, motives and ideologies, rules and laws, institutions and industries, power and money—all of these topics have a role to play in cybersecurity, and all of these are tightly interwoven.

The *SpringerBriefs in Cybersecurity* series is comprised of two types of briefs: topic- and country-specific briefs. Topic-specific briefs strive to provide a comprehensive coverage of the whole range of topics surrounding cybersecurity, combining whenever possible legal, ethical, social, political and technical issues. Authors with diverse backgrounds explain their motivation, their mindset, and their approach to the topic, to illuminate its theoretical foundations, the practical nuts and bolts and its past, present and future. Country-specific briefs cover national perceptions and strategies, with officials and national authorities explaining the background, the leading thoughts and interests behind the official statements, to foster a more informed international dialogue.

More information about this series at http://www.springer.com/series/10634

Aamo Iorliam

Cybersecurity in Nigeria

A Case Study of Surveillance and Prevention
of Digital Crime

 Springer

Aamo Iorliam
Department of Mathematics
and Computer Science
Benue State University
Makurdi, Nigeria

ISSN 2193-973X   ISSN 2193-9748 (electronic)
SpringerBriefs in Cybersecurity
ISBN 978-3-030-15209-3   ISBN 978-3-030-15210-9 (eBook)
https://doi.org/10.1007/978-3-030-15210-9

Library of Congress Control Number: 2019933714

This Springer imprint is published by the registered company Springer Nature Switzerland AG
The registered company address is: Gewerbestrasse 11, 6330 Cham, Switzerland

To God Almighty

Foreword

This five-chapter book titled Cybersecurity in Nigeria—A Case Study of Surveillance and Prevention of Digital Crime by Dr. Iorliam is a handbook containing all you need to know about cyber surveillance in Nigeria. It looks at how cyber surveillance could stop digital crimes in Nigeria and by extension the world.

The author knows his stuff, having earned an M.Sc. in Forensic Computing with a distinction from Coventry University and a Ph.D. in Computer Science with a thesis focusing on the Application of Power Laws to Biometrics, Forensics and Network Traffic Analysis from the University of Surrey, both in UK. From these universities, he was able to sharpen and cut his academic teeth.

The book demonstrates his knowledge of his research areas which include Power laws, machine learning, data mining, image analysis, digital and multimedia forensics, cybersecurity, biometrics, computer forensics and network traffic analysis.

From his research standpoint, the author delved into areas of the application of forensic science to solve problems in network traffic analysis, fake news detection and the development of a digital surveillance software to prevent/detect digitally facilitated crimes in Nigeria.

This book is divided into five chapters;

Chapter 1 provides the necessary introduction that a reader needs to be able to understand and get the best out of the book.

Chapter 2 shows how Natural laws can effectively detect malicious traffic on the Internet.

Chapter 3 shows how Natural laws can solve a very important challenge in Nigeria—fake news detection.

Chapter 4 provides an explanation to how cyber crimes occur in Nigeria and the need for cybersecurity and mobile device forensics to solve this challenge.

Chapter 5 proposes a digital surveillance software (A-BOT) that can effectively stop digital crimes in Nigeria.

This book is a must read for forensic scientists, cryptographers, stenographers and all law enforcement agencies in Nigeria. It is a gift from Dr. Iorliam to a world in dire need of the knowledge on the secrets of forensic science in solving different types of crimes. I strongly recommend this book to you!

Lokoja, Nigeria   Prof. Sunday Eric Adewumi, Ph.D., fncs
January 2019   Dean, Faculty of Science
                                                                  Federal University Lokoja

Preface

It is not new that the Nigerian cyber space and its cyber infrastructure is very porous and has given much room to cyber attackers to freely operate. In 2017, 3500 cyber attacks on the Nigerian cyber space were successful. This led to Nigeria losing 450 million dollars [1].

These cyber crimes are hampering Nigeria's digital economy. This further explains why many Nigerians are not convinced about Internet marketing and online transactions that involve money. This is worrisome even for the Nigerian military intelligence. If sensitive conversations using digital devices (e.g. phones or computers) are not well monitored, then Nigeria will be defeated in the cyber warfare. If Nigeria loses the cyber warfare, then our digital economy, military intelligence and related sensitive firms will also crumble.

The Nigerian Army Cyber Warfare Command was instituted in 2018 with a task to solve terrorism, banditry and other attacks by criminal groups in Nigeria [2]. This is a right step by the Nigerian government. However, there is every need to provide digital surveillance to the Nigerian cyber space to assist law enforcement agencies in Nigeria to prevent/detect these digitally facilitated crimes.

Therefore, monitoring of Nigeria's cyber space and its cyber infrastructure has become imperative given that the rate of criminal activities has increased tremendously using technology. Cyber infrastructure consists of computing systems, data storage systems, advanced instruments and data repositories, visualization environments and people, all linked by high-speed networks to make possible scholarly innovation and discoveries not otherwise possible. Information technology systems that provide particularly powerful and advanced capabilities could also be referred to as cyber infrastructure [3]. This book proposes the use of digital surveillance aimed at investigating, detecting, uncovering and interpreting any fraud associated with the cyber space and critical cyber infrastructures in Nigeria. This will make the Nigerian digital ecosystem free of cyber attackers. This digital surveillance includes passive forensic investigations (investigations where an attack has already occurred) and active forensic investigations (real-time investigations to track attackers). Hence, producing a zero-cyber crime Nigeria.

Makurdi, Nigeria   Dr. Aamo Iorliam
January 2019

References

1. The Paradigm (2017) Nigerias cyberspace has become very porous-senate. http://www.theparadigmng.com/2017/05/24/nigerias-cyberspace-become-porous-senate/. Accessed 27 Nov 2018
2. Sunnewsonline (2018) Insurgency: army establishes cyber warfare command. http://sunnewsonline.com/insurgency-army-establishes-cyber-warfare-command/. Accessed 27 Nov 2018
3. Indiana University (2018) What is cyberinfrastructure?. https://kb.iu.edu/d/auhf. Accessed 27 Nov 2018

Acknowledgements

Special thanks to the following:

- Springer Team: For your support towards making the publication of this book a huge success.
- My Ph.D. supervisors: Prof. Anthony T. S. Ho, Prof. Shujun Li, Dr. Norman Poh and Prof. Adrian Waller who mentored me.
- To my friends: Dr. Santosh Tirunagari, Shangbum Caleb Faveren, Dr. Nyinoh Iveren, Oshido Barnabas, Ode Egena, Dr. Ikyanyon Darius.
- To my family members: Mr. and Mrs. Iorliam (Dad and Mum), Eng. Dr. and Dr. (Mrs.) Yala Iorliam, Pastor and Mrs. Aondowase Tsuaa, Mr. and Barr. (Mrs.) Nguetar Iorliam, Mr. and Mrs. Ukaan.
  And most importantly, my wife Iveren (Udookwase), and my two daughters, Afam and Asoose, who supported and encouraged me throughout the whole process of writing this book.

Contents

1 **Introduction** 1
  1.1 Main Contributions 1
  1.2 Document Structure 2

2 **Natural Laws (Benford's Law and Zipf's Law) for Network**
  Traffic Analysis 3
  2.1 Contribution 4
  2.2 Benford's Law 4
  2.3 Zipf's Law 6
  2.4 Network Traffic Analysis and IDS 6
    2.4.1 Flow-Based IDS 7
  2.5 Network Flows and TCP Flows 8
  2.6 Application to Network Traffic Analysis 9
    2.6.1 Method Description 9
    2.6.2 The Metrics 9
    2.6.3 Analysis of Different Flow Ordering Options 10
  2.7 Experimental Setup and Results 11
    2.7.1 Datasets Used for Our Experiments 11
    2.7.2 Flow Size or Flow Size Difference 12
    2.7.3 How to Determine Flow Window Size 12
    2.7.4 TCP Flow Ordering 13
    2.7.5 More Results on Different Datasets 13
    2.7.6 Zipf's Law for Network Traffic Analysis 14
    2.7.7 Zipf's Law for Malicious, Non-malicious, Mixture
       of Malicious and Non-malicious Network Traffic 16
    2.7.8 Comparative Analysis of Zipf's Law and Benford's
       Law with Implications 17
  2.8 Conclusion 20
  References 20

**3   Combination of Natural Laws (Benford's Law and Zipf's Law)
     for Fake News Detection**   23
   3.1   Combination of Benford's Law and Zipf's Law for Fake
          News Detection   24
   3.2   Results and Discussions   29
   3.3   Conclusion   29
   References   30

4   Cybersecurity and Mobile Device Forensic   31
   4.1   Nigeria and Internet Fraud   32
   4.2   Reasons for Increase in Cyber Crimes in Nigeria   34
   4.3   Types of Cyber Crimes in Nigeria   35
   4.4   Link Between Mobile Device Forensics and Cybersecurity   37
   4.5   Cybersecurity Laws and Punishment in Nigeria   40
   4.6   Conclusion   42
   References   43

5   Proposed Digital Surveillance Software   45
   5.1   Introduction   45
   5.2   System Analysis and Design   49
   5.3   Product Features and How It Works   49
   5.4   The Solution (A-BOT)   52
   5.5   Advantages of the Proposed System   54
   5.6   Conclusion   55
   References   55

Chapter 1
Introduction

Nigeria has recorded a tremendous increase in digitally facilitated crimes. This is due to the improper surveillance of Nigeria's digital space and lack of forensic experts/tools. As such, Nigeria has high cyber attacks vulnerability index in Africa and several billions of Naira is lost to cyber crime annually. If nothing is done to curb these crimes, they will keep increasing and Nigeria will keep loosing huge amounts to cyber crimes.

This book investigates passive and active forensic techniques that could be applied to the Nigerian cyber space to curb digitally facilitated crimes. To better understand the most suitable passive forensic approaches for cyber surveillance in Nigeria, a comparative analysis is performed between Zipf's law and Benford's law. Furthermore, a combination of Benford's law and Zipf's law is proposed for the detection of fake news in Nigeria. Again, cyber security and mobile device forensics and how it relates to Nigeria is properly presented. This book proposes the development of a sophisticated digital surveillance software (A-BOT) well tailored for the Nigerian digital space to prevent/detect crimes on digital devices. By digital surveillance software, we mean software that could be remotely installed on suspects/attackers digital devices (e.g. phones, computers) for capturing forensic evidence.

1.1 Main Contributions

The main contributions made in this work are the following:

- The application and analysis of Power laws (Benford's law and Zipf's law) to detect malicious traffic on the Internet.
- The combination of Benford's law and Zipf's law for fake news detection is proposed.

© The Author(s), under exclusive license to Springer Nature Switzerland AG 2019
A. Iorliam, *Cybersecurity in Nigeria*, SpringerBriefs in Cybersecurity,
https://doi.org/10.1007/978-3-030-15210-9_1

- The evaluation of cybersecurity challenges is presented. Furthermore, cybersecurity and mobile device forensics for Nigerian cyber space and digital devices are discussed.
- The proposed digital surveillance software (A-BOT) is recommended to curb digitally facilitated crimes in Nigeria.

1.2 Document Structure

This document is organized as follows:

- Chapter 2 investigates the application of Natural laws (Benford's law and Zipf's law) for network traffic analysis. This chapter further recommends the deployment of these two laws for network traffic analysis in Nigeria.
- Chapter 3 proposes a novel combination of Natural Laws (Benford's law and Zipf's law) for fake news detection.
- Chapter 4 carefully investigates cyber crimes committed in Nigeria. The chapter also reviews mobile device forensic tools and how these tools could be used in Nigeria to prevent/detect digitally facilitated crimes. Furthermore, the chapter emphasizes the need for cybersecurity and mobile device forensics in Nigeria.
- Chapter 5 proposes a novel digital surveillance software (A-BOT) that could be used in preventing/detecting digitally facilitated crimes in Nigeria.

Chapter 2
Natural Laws (Benford's Law and Zipf's Law) for Network Traffic Analysis

Abstract Recently, Benford's law and Zipf's law, which are both statistical laws, have been effectively used to distinguish between authentic data and fake data. Some similarities that exist between Benford's law and Zipf's law are that both of these laws are classified as natural laws. Also, both laws are Power laws and it is expected that distributions that follow Benford's law should also follow Zipf's law. Even though both laws have similarities, there exist some differences between these two laws. Benford's law establishes a relationship between digit and frequency. In contrast, Zipf's law shows a relationship between rank and frequency. Another difference that exists between these two laws is that Benford's law applies to numeric attributes, whereas Zipf's law applies to both numeric and string attributes. In this chapter, we perform a comparative analysis of these two laws on network traffic data and to determine whether they follow these laws and discriminate between non-malicious and malicious network traffic flows. We observe that both the laws effectively detected whether a particular network was non-malicious or malicious by investigating its data using these laws. Furthermore, we observe that the initial Benford's law chi-square divergence values obtained seem to be inversely proportional to Zipf's law P-values, which can be potentially exploited for intrusion detection system applications. These passive forensic detection methods when properly deployed to analyse network traffic data in Nigeria will save the Nigerian cyber space from malware and related attacks.

Keywords Benford's law · Zipf's law · Network traffic analysis · Cyber space

Statistical characteristics of network traffic have recently attracted a significant amount of research interest due to the rich amount of information transmitted over the Internet. Using Benford's law and Zipf's law for statistical analysis of network traffic is one way to detect malicious traffic on the Internet. Distributions such as the intensity of earthquakes [1], population of cities [2], number of visitors to a site, number of hyperlinks to a web page [3] and TCP flow inter-arrival times [4] have been found to follow a Power law (in which Benford's law and Zipf's law are classified as one of the Power laws). Prior work on the statistical analysis of network traffic using Power laws have been carried out by Faloutsos et al. [5], Mahanti et al. [3] and van Mierlo et al. [6]. Faloutsos et al. [5] showed that the Power law holds for snapshots of the Internet between November 1997 and December 1998. Mahanti et al. [3] reviewed how the Power law has improved the design and performance of Internet-based systems. Furthermore, they stated some implications of using Power laws in computer networks. Such implications include the use of Power laws in web caching, search schemes, business practices, system designs and measurement issues with respect to the authenticity of Power laws. van Mierlo et al. [6] showed that mechanisms of digital healthcare social networks follow a Power law. This has an application in helping managers in establishing budgets and expenditures in a healthcare setting. However, to the best of our knowledge, a comparative analysis of Benford's law and Zipf's law for network traffic metrics such as flow size and flow size difference has not been previously investigated.

2.1 Contribution

Benford's law and Zipf's law have proved to be very effective in different disciplines. Therefore, our novel contribution in this chapter is to investigate the application of these laws on network traffic data and perform a comparative analysis of how effective they work in detecting malicious traffic on the Internet. In this chapter, we answer the following questions:

- Is Benford's law applicable to TCP flow size difference of network traffic data?
- Can the TCP flow size difference of network traffic data assist in detecting malicious traffic on the Internet?
- Is Zipf's law applicable to TCP flow size difference of network traffic data?
- Does network traffic data behave the same way for Benford's law and Zipf's law?

The remainder of the chapter is as follows: In Sect. 2.2, we explain the concept of Benford's law. Section 2.3 explains the concept of Zipf's law. Network traffic analysis and intrusion detection systems are covered in Sect. 2.4. In Sect. 2.5, network flows and TCP flows are properly covered. Application of our proposed method to network traffic analysis is covered in Sect. 2.6. Experimental Setup and Results are discussed in Sect. 2.7. Finally, in Sect. 2.8, we draw conclusions.

2.2 Benford's Law

Benford's law has been reported by Fu et al. [7], Li et al. [8] and Xu et al. [9] to be very effective in detecting tampering of images. Benford's law of 'anomalous digits' was coined by Frank Benford in 1938 [10], which is also described as the first digit law considers the frequency of appearance of the most significant digit (MSD), for a broad range of natural and artificial data [11]. Benford's law as described by Hill [12] can be expressed in the form of a logarithmic distribution, when considering the probability distribution of the first digit from 1 to 9 for a range of natural data. Naturally generated

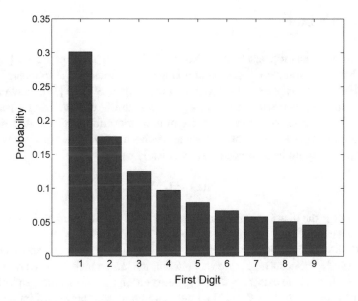

Fig. 2.1 The first digit probability distribution of Benford's law

data are supposed to obey this law, whereas tampered or randomly guessed data are supposed to disobey this law [13].

When considering the MSD where 0 is excluded, and the datasets satisfy Benford's law, then the law can be expressed as Eq. (2.1) [12].

$$P(x) = \log_{10}(1 + \frac{1}{x}) \tag{2.1}$$

where x is the first digit of the number and $P(x)$ refers to the probability distribution of x. The first digit probability distribution of Benford's law is shown in Fig. 2.1.

An extension of Benford's law by Fu et al. [7] is referred to represent a generalized Benford's law, which closely follows a logarithmic law is defined in Eq. (2.2) [7].

$$P(x) = N \log_{10}(1 + \frac{1}{s + x^q}) \tag{2.2}$$

where N is a normalization factor which makes $P(x)$ a probability distribution. The model parameters in this case are represented by s and q which describe the distributions for different images and different compressions QFs as defined in [7]. Through experiments, Fu et al. [7] provided values for N, s and q. They determined these values using the MATLAB toolbox, which returns the Sum of Squares due to Error (SSE).

2.3 Zipf's Law

Zipf's law was first proposed by American Linguist George K. Zipf in 1935 [14]. Zipf stated that given some corpus of natural language utterances, the frequency of any word is inversely proportional to its rank in the frequency table [14]. Newman [15] further explained that when considering the probability of measuring a particular quantity (in our case, flow size difference of network traffic data) and such quantity varies inversely as a power of that value, such quantity is said to follow Zipf's law [15]. This could be expressed mathematically as

$$p(x) = Cx^{-\alpha} \tag{2.3}$$

where $p(x)$ is the distribution of the quantity x, α is the exponent of Zipf's law and C is a constant [15].

Zipf's law is considered as a Power law, because small occurrences are very common and large occurrences are very uncommon [15], which depicts the definition of a Power law. There exist a relationship between Zipf's law and the Benford's law. Toa [16] and Christelli et al. [17] all noted a relationship between Zipf's law and Benford's law. They found that these laws hold true when the following conditions are fulfilled:

- All values as positive numbers;
- Variables significantly differ in magnitude;
- Statistics arise from a complicated combination of largely independent factors;
- Variables are not artificially rounded, truncated or constrained in size [16, 17].

Since the first publication on Power laws, a number of natural phenomena have been found to follow the Power laws. These include the frequency of words used in any human language [15], the population of cities [15, 18], the intensity of earthquakes [15, 18], sizes of power outages [18] and the ranks of people watching a particular TV station at a time [15] amongst others.

Huang et al. [19] used Zipf's law to detect a source of suspicion using intrusion detection datasets and showed that it could assist in the auditing process. They showed that Zipf's law could distinguish between normal and abnormal data from an intrusion detection system on networks [19]. Both Benford's law and Zipf's law have been used to assist in detecting anomalies [15]. Iorliam et al. [20] used Benford's law and Zipf's law for the analysis of keystroke data to discriminate between humans using keystroke biometric systems from non-humans.

2.4 Network Traffic Analysis and IDS

Krugel et al. [21] defined Intrusion Detection (ID) as the process of identifying and responding to malicious activities targeted at computing and network resources. Sperotto and Pras [22] classified IDS systems into misuse based or anomaly based.

Both misuse-based IDS and anomaly-based IDS have advantages and disadvantages. Even though misuse-based IDS has the advantage of being accurate, it cannot detect new attacks. This is because the misuse-based IDS works by using an already prede-fined set of rules from previous intrusion scenarios and new attacks usually have a different signature, hence bypassing these systems. In contrast, anomaly-based IDS can potentially detect even new attacks, however, it has a disadvantage of classify-ing some deviations that are not malicious as malicious [22]. Due to the advantages exhibited by anomaly-based IDS, it is a preferred approach for IDS research and development [4]. Anomaly-based techniques are classified into statistically based, knowledge based and machine based [23]. For statistically based approaches, they are either packet-based or flow-based methods. A detailed review by Bhuyan et al. [24] described several packet-based approaches such as the use of learned prob-ability distribution to detect anomaly over noisy data [25], the use of rule learning algorithm and clustering algorithm to identify normal behaviour and also outliers for anomaly detection [26], and the classification of network traffic patterns based on generalized likelihood ratio test for anomaly detection [27]. All of these examples are packet-based methods for IDS. However, Bhuyan et al. [24] noted that only a single research carried out by Lu and Ghorbani [28] used both packet-based and flow-based approaches with wavelet analysis as a detection method. Power laws are also referred to as 'natural' laws, because many natural processes often follow them while artificially created ones tend not to. Since attacks are normally artificially crafted and mostly generate 'unnatural' network traffic, those natural laws can often form the basis (or part) of an anomaly-based IDS.

2.4.1 Flow-Based IDS

One of the major challenges faced by IDS systems is related to the handling of high volumes of data due to today's high-speed network [22]. In view of this chal-lenge, Sperotto and Pras [22] and Bejtlich [29] suggested the use of flow-based approaches for IDS purposes, which consumed less amount of resources than packet-based approaches which required high resource consumption [22, 29]. We also use flow-based approach with the aim of investigating the possibility of detecting attacks using the flow size of network traffic.

Steinberger et al. stated that flow-based anomaly detection systems are not com-monly used [30]. Lakhina et al. used Principal Component Analysis to diagnose network-wide traffic anomalies [31]. There are IDS methods [22] developed for net-work traffic analysis. However, the attackers are constantly evolving their methods and are able to bypass many of the existing methods. The important distinguishing feature of our research discussed in this chapter is the investigation of a new net-work flow metric 'flow size difference', using Benford's law and Zipf's law for IDS purposes.

2.5   Network Flows and TCP Flows

A network flow, which may sometimes be called a session, a stream or a conversation, is a sequence of network packets sharing some common criteria such as two endpoint IP addresses over the Internet [29]. In principle, the network flow concept can be applied to any network protocol at any layer of a network.

While there are many different ways to define a network flow, one of the most common definition uses the following five criteria: source and destination IP addresses, source and destination port numbers (0 for protocols that do not use ports) and protocol type. When we talk about 'source' and 'destination', it is clear that the flow defined is unidirectional, which is the case for NetFlow and IPFIX flows. However, as Bejtlich pointed out in [29], connection-oriented protocols (e.g. TCP) are more suited to be represented as a flow as compared to connectionless protocols (e.g. IP, UDP and ICMP). This is because the former are structured in such a way that there exists a clear beginning, middle and end to a TCP session, whereas the latter are not structured around the concept of connections, so often time expiration conditions have to be used to arbitrarily set flow boundaries. For connection-oriented protocols, each connection corresponds to a bidirectional flow which is the merging of the two unidirectional flows.

In flow-based IDSs, different flow definitions are used. IP flows defined following NetFlow or IPFIX specifications are widely used since such flow information can often be obtained directly from routers and supported by open-source tools such as NFDUMP and NfSen. Some researchers focused on bidirectional TCP flows only [4], which can be justified by the fact that most IP traffic over the Internet is TCP traffic.

In this chapter, we also focused on bidirectional TCP flows as Arshadi and Jahangir did in their work on [4] considering the dominance of TCP flows on the Internet and the fact that network flows are less well-defined for IP and other connectionless protocols. Note that selecting TCP flows naturally cover all application-layer protocols based on TCP (such as HTTP, the dominating protocol at the application layer).

When working with a pcap file captured by *libpacap* or *WinPcap*, the TCP flows we work with can be generated using the following command line with *tshark* (a command-line utility provided with *WireShark*): tshark -r < input pcap file > -q -z conv,tcp > <output file>. The output file will then contain a list of 'TCP conversations', which is a term used by *WireShark* to denote TCP flows.[1] In *WireShark*'s user interface, TCP flows of a given network traffic dataset can be obtained via the menu item 'Statistics' → 'Conversation' and then click 'TCP' tab. Then the TCP flows shown in the interface can be exported using 'Copy' button at the bottom. The TCP flow obtained this way contains the following attributes (those in boldface are essential for our work): source IP address, source port number, destination IP address, destination port number, **total number of packets transferred between source and destination, total number of bytes transferred**

---

[1] *WireShark* uses another term 'TCP stream' to denote the payload of a 'TCP conversation'. To avoid confusion, we will use the term 'TCP flow' consistently in this chapter.

between source and destination, packets transferred from source to destination, bytes transferred from source to destination, packets transferred from destination to source, bytes transferred from destination to source, **relative start time** (as a timestamp, 0 = the beginning of the whole network traffic), **duration**, source-to-destination bitrate (bit per second) and destination-to-source bitrate. When working with other network traffic data, as long as we can extract the above attributes of each TCP flow in boldface, our proposed method will work without any problem.

2.6 Application to Network Traffic Analysis

2.6.1 Method Description

There are currently a few proposed statistical approaches for network traffic anomalies [4]. Arshadi and Jahangir [4] showed that Benford's law could be applied to the inter-arrival times of TCP for normal traffic and a deviation could be considered as an anomaly. In this chapter, we consider the typical structure of an anomaly-based IDS working with TCP flows. Our approach starts with one or more selected metrics which should follow Benford's law closely for normal TCP flows but deviate from it significantly and consistently for malicious ones. Therefore, the flow size difference will be investigated using Benford's law and Zipf's law to detect malicious traffic on the Internet.

2.6.2 The Metrics

Since we aim at identifying new metrics, we do not look at the inter-arrival time already studied by other researchers [4]. We identify two candidate metrics that have not been previously studied for IDS:

Flow size: The flow size distribution has been studied extensively in the networking literature and estimation of flow size distribution has been an active research topic [32]. We were unaware of work linking flow size distribution to Benford's law and Zipf's law so found it interesting to investigate flow size as a new metric for applying Benford's law and Zipf's law.

Flow size difference: In addition to flow size, we also found 'flow size difference', which is defined as the numeric difference of two consecutive TCP flows' sizes, seems to be another candidate metric of interest because it inherits some features of flow size (e.g. long-tailedness) but also differs significantly from flow size itself. We did not find any work on the distribution of flow size difference of TCP flows or on its application in IDS. However, our initial experiments revealed that it seemed to follow Benford's law, so we added it as a candidate. For flow size difference, we ignore the sign bit so the metric we are considering here is actually the absolute value of the flow size difference. In the following, we simply use the term 'flow size difference' to denote the absolute value unless otherwise stated.

Note that the flow size can be defined by bytes or packets, so we actually have two different variants for each of the above two metrics. These two variants are not linked but cannot be directly derived from each other since the packet size (in byte) varies over time and across applications. Therefore, we use two different variants of the flow size difference metric (flow size as number of bytes and number of packets) in this chapter.

2.6.3 Analysis of Different Flow Ordering Options

For flow size difference, changing ordering of flows will obviously change each sample of the metric and thus its observed distribution. For flow size, ordering will not make a direct difference, but can influence what flows are included in each flow window thus affecting the observed distribution. It is, therefore, a valid question to ask whether such ordering will make a difference. If so, how we should order flows. Looking at all the attributes of a TCP flow, we select the following four typical ordering options for consideration:

1. Start Time, End Time: This ordering criterion considers both the start time and end time of a flow.
2. End Time, Start Time: This ordering criterion considers both the end time and start time of a flow.
3. Source IP address, Source Port number, Destination IP address, Destination Port number, Start Time: This is a 5-tuple ordering criterion which considers source IP address, source port number, destination IP address, destination port number and start time of a flow.
4. Source IP address, Destination IP address, Start Time: This ordering criterion considers the source IP address, destination IP address and start time of a flow.

Each attribute in the above ordering option is considered from left to right for ordering. When some flows have the same values for all ordering criteria, the original order in the raw network traffic log will be kept. Since Benford's law and Zipf's law are natural laws, we hypothesize that the ordering should not have a significant impact on the compliance with (for normal flows) or deviation from (for malicious flows) Benford's law and Zipf's law. Our experimental results will be given in Sect. 2.7.

2.7 Experimental Setup and Results

2.7.1 Datasets Used for Our Experiments

To properly test the new metrics, we use three groups of network traffic datasets in our experiments. The first group are datasets that do not contain known malicious traffic (so considered as normal/non-malicious). The second group are datasets containing known malicious traffic. The third group are datasets with unlabelled mixed traffic with both malicious and non-malicious flows. All datasets were preprocessed using *tshark* to get bidirectional TCP flows.

Non-malicious traffic datasets considered in our experiments include the following:

1. LBNL and ICSI dataset [33]: This dataset has packets spanned for more than 100 hours of activity from a total of several thousand internal hosts.
2. UNB ISCX 2012 Intrusion Detection Dataset: We consider two datasets here that are non-malicious. Traffic on Friday (11/6/2010) has normal activity and non-malicious flows with 297,398 TCP flows. Second, traffic on Wednesday (16/6/2010) also has normal activity and non-malicious flows with 434,674 TCP flows [34].
3. TLERH dataset: This dataset has captured data volume of 6 Gbytes, for a duration of 43 hours that contains 12 million packets [35].
4. Other publicly available non-malicious traffic datasets used in our experiments are from PCAP traces [36].

The malicious datasets considered in our experiments include the following:

1. Capture hacker dataset: We use captured malware traffic of three honeypot PCAP files with different setups namely NAPENTHES, HONEYBOT and AMA-ZON [37].
2. 2009 CDX dataset: This dataset includes packet captures generated by National Security Agency (NSA) Red Team activity [38].
3. MACCDC dataset: This dataset has normal flows with periodic attacks from a volunteer Red Team. We randomly picked 4 pcap files from this repository [39].
4. Labelled dataset for intrusion detection: The dataset has honeypot flow information of traffic in the network of the University of Twente [40].
5. Kyoto University Benchmark Data: It has 24 statistical features; 14 conventional features and 10 additional features. 14 of these features are extracted based on KDD Cup 99 dataset, which are basically obtained by honeypot systems [41].

The first unlabelled mixed datasets of non-malicious and malicious traffic used for our experiments are from UNB ISCX 2012 intrusion detection dataset. They include data traffics of the following:

- Sunday (13/6/2010) which has 221,026 TCP flows with 20,358 attacked flows.
- Monday (14/6/2010) which has 122,298 TCP flows with 3,771 attacked flows.

Table 2.1 χ^2 divergence values for flow size versus flow size difference as the metric

Dataset (File)	Metric	
	Flow size	Flow size difference
LBNL/ICSI	0.23211	0.00789
Capture hacker (HONEYBOT)	1.09218	0.35986
ISCX 2012 (13/06/2012)	0.69808	0.02574

- Tuesday (15/6/2010) which has 441,563 TCP flows with 37,378 attached flows.
- Thursday (17/6/ 2010) which has 329,378 TCP flows with 5,203 attacked flows [34].

The second mixed dataset is ISOT dataset, which comprises of existing publicly available malicious and non-malicious datasets [42].

2.7.2 Flow Size or Flow Size Difference

The first phase of the experiment we conducted is to determine if both flow size and flow size difference are promising metrics for IDS purposes. We use one dataset from each of the three groups to gain insights about their potentials. Table 2.1 summarizes the results, which show that flow size difference seems to follow Benford's law better than flow size although for both cases the expected order of the χ^2 divergence values were observed: non-malicious < mixed < malicious. We also repeat this experiment with some other datasets and observed largely the same pattern, therefore we decide to choose flow size difference for other experiments.

2.7.3 How to Determine Flow Window Size

Since Benford's law and Zipf's law are distributions, we need to collect a sufficient number of samples of a given metric to be able to construct an observed distribution which then can be compared against the target distribution for detecting deviation. The flow window size W is a parameter of the IDS which can allow some level of performance control. While we expect that W does not need to be too large, nevertheless, we need some indication of how we can set it. For a selected dataset (LBNL/ICSI dataset), we thus calculated the average χ^2 divergence value of all flows when the flow window size W changes from 500 to 20,000, increasing with a step size of 250. Figure 2.2 shows the results. As can be seen, the average χ^2 divergence value decreases rapidly initially but the decreasing rate keeps dropping while W increases. Note that the initial divergence value is also very small (below 0.02), so the results suggest W can probably be set to a value between several hundred or thousand in most cases.

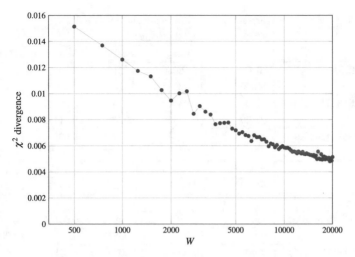

Fig. 2.2 Change of χ^2 divergence w.r.t. flow window size W

2.7.4 TCP Flow Ordering

In this section, the ordering of flows will be investigated to see whether it has an effect on how flow size difference follows the Benford's law. For non-malicious flows in the LBNL/ICSI dataset, the average χ^2 divergence values for all four ordering options listed in Sect. 2.6.3 are: 0.03354, 0.03416, 0.03192 and 0.03362, all below 0.03. For malicious flows in the HONEYBOT dataset, the average χ^2 divergence values are 0.36906, 0.35287, 0.33000 and 0.35663, all above 0.3. Repeated experiments on other malicious and non-malicious datasets gave similar results, so we can see that the flow ordering does not really change the χ^2 divergence value, thus suggesting that flow size difference is a robust metric against flow ordering.

2.7.5 More Results on Different Datasets

The above experiments clarified that flow size difference is a good metric working with Benford's law. To test its potential further, we ran a large-scale experiment to calculate χ^2 divergence values for a large number of TCP flows of many datasets in all the three groups. Tables 2.2, 2.3 and 2.4 show the results for the three different groups of datasets, respectively. Note that the χ^2 divergence values of different datasets should be compared directly as those datasets correspond to completely different networking environments and capturing methods. Despite the diversity of the datasets and the observable fluctuations of the χ^2 divergence values especially the maximum values, largely speaking the χ^2 divergence value does have a high tendency to follow the following order: non-malicious < mixed < malicious. This suggests flow size difference may indeed be a good metric for building an anomaly-based IDS for detecting malicious flows.

Table 2.2 χ^2 divergence values for datasets with non-malicious TCP flows

Dataset (File)	Window size	χ^2 divergence			
		Average	Median	Minimum	Maximum
LBNL/ICSI	2000	0.06086	0.02194	0.00036	3.73021
	10000	0.02335	0.01453	0.00079	0.14223
ISCX 2012 (11/6/2010)	2000	0.03548	0.03078	0.00531	0.11843
	10000	0.02468	0.02424	0.01413	0.03884
ISCX 2012 (16/6/2010)	2000	0.07623	0.03926	0.00144	0.78547
	10000	0.04398	0.03093	0.00373	0.18447
TLERH	2000	0.06206	0.04660	0.00877	0.17518
	10000	0.04680	0.04573	0.03653	0.05830
Pcap Traces					
(loc1-20020523-1835)	2000	0.01057	0.00896	0.00126	0.03748
	10000	0.00530	0.00528	0.00252	0.00921
(loc1-20020524-1115)	2000	0.00863	0.00792	0.00170	0.02550
	10000	0.00321	0.00298	0.00105	0.00653
(loc2-20030513-1005)	2000	0.01727	0.01570	0.00310	0.05432
	10000	0.00691	0.00691	0.00691	0.00691
(loc2-20030513-1044)	2000	0.04595	0.04072	0.01591	0.09965
	10000	0.02966	0.02966	0.02966	0.02966
(loc3-20030902-0930)	2000	0.01848	0.01758	0.00430	0.03842
	10000	0.01234	0.01264	0.00855	0.01662
(loc3-20030902-1005)	2000	0.01574	0.01576	0.00275	0.03699
	10000	0.01137	0.01141	0.00648	0.01682
(loc4-20040204-2145)	2000	0.01770	0.01737	0.00115	0.04557
	10000	0.01317	0.01434	0.00137	0.02149
(loc4-20040205-0410)	2000	0.01998	0.01925	0.00238	0.05784
	10000	0.01512	0.01632	0.00123	0.02550
(loc5-20031205-1431)	2000	0.04746	0.04571	0.01340	0.09680
	10000	0.04198	0.04207	0.03003	0.05681
(loc5-20031206-0731)	2000	0.08954	0.08395	0.04891	0.18042
	10000	0.07028	0.07102	0.06119	0.07695
(loc6-20070501-2055)	2000	0.06028	0.04257	0.00312	0.74296
	10000	0.04050	0.03623	0.01130	0.14532
(loc6-20070531-2043)	2000	0.06458	0.04797	0.00358	0.90895
	10000	0.04812	0.03955	0.00907	0.19312

2.7.6 Zipf's Law for Network Traffic Analysis

Benford's law is the most used Power law when dealing with fraud detection [19]. A related Power law to the Benford's law is Zipf's law. Some similarities that exist between Benford's law and Zipf's law are that both of these laws are classified

Table 2.3 χ^2 divergence values for datasets with malicious TCP flows

Dataset (File)	Window size	χ^2 divergence			
		Average	Median	Minimum	Maximum
Capture Hacker					
(HONEYBOT)	2000	0.35986	0.35986	0.35986	0.35986
(AMAZON)	2000	0.54118	0.66649	0.29142	0.77195
(NAPENTHES)	2000	0.77923	0.77923	0.77923	0.77923
2009 *CDX*					
(dmp1)	2000	0.41638	0.39082	0.15523	0.69919
(dmp2)	2000	0.53069	0.45369	0.23580	1.03266
(dmp3)	2000	1.28681	0.54223	0.14934	8.28480
(dmp4)	2000	0.60792	0.57368	0.24486	1.23878
(35dump)	2000	3.59944	1.08522	0.05952	12.11948
(35dump2)	2000	0.53069	0.45369	0.23580	1.03266
MACCDC					
(MACC1)	2000	0.56174	0.49859	0.03080	2.47686
	10000	0.36168	0.30968	0.09280	0.66531
(MACC2)	2000	0.31569	0.34896	0.04497	0.73550
	10000	0.30172	0.33339	0.07782	0.47961
(MACC3)	2000	0.48010	0.51602	0.07955	1.34011
	10000	0.27954	0.27954	0.27954	0.27954
(MACC4)	2000	0.45209	0.41458	0.02987	1.60890
	10000	0.31705	0.24440	0.04732	0.91747
Labelled flows	2000	1.01993	0.90067	0.03410	3.79592
	10000	0.99995	0.88509	0.07798	3.58846
Kyoto					
(20061101)	2000	0.10674	0.09805	0.02955	0.22716
(20061102)	2000	1.06613	1.00048	0.09981	3.15303
(20061103)	2000	0.10819	0.11279	0.05818	0.19531
(20061104)	2000	0.36946	0.44474	0.07109	0.61212

as natural laws [19]. Also, both laws are Power laws [19] and it is expected that distributions that follow Benford's law should also follow Zipf's law. Even though both laws have similarities, there exist some differences between these two laws. Benford's law establishes a relationship between digit and frequency. In contrast, Zipf's law shows a relationship between rank and frequency. Another difference that exists between these two laws is that Benford's law applies to numeric attributes, whereas Zipf's law applies to both numeric and string attributes [19].

Our assumption in this section is that the TCP flow size difference from non-malicious flows should also follow Zipf's law and that TCP flow size difference from malicious flows should deviate from Zipf's law. For our experiments, we use

Table 2.4 χ^2 divergence values for datasets with mixed malicious and non-malicious TCP flows

Dataset (File)	Window size	χ^2 divergence			
		Average	Median	Minimum	Maximum
ISCX 2012					
(13/6/2010)	2000	0.37707	0.08137	0.00190	5.87357
	10000	0.20355	0.06338	0.01177	2.26241
(14/6/2010)	2000	0.20078	0.04725	0.00361	3.63736
	10000	0.10629	0.03444	0.00806	1.01057
(15/6/2010)	2000	0.12120	0.08677	0.00300	1.19159
	10000	0.09664	0.07293	0.00825	0.56655
(17/6/2010)	2000	0.06915	0.059462	0.00734	0.32674
	10000	0.04617	0.04309	0.01686	0.09487
ISOT	2000	0.05151	0.02077	0.00090	1.52625
	10000	0.01931	0.01380	0.00084	0.41024

the TCP flow size difference from malicious dataset (capture the hacker, 2009 CDX dataset-35 dump, 2009 CDX dataset-35 dump2), non-malicious dataset (LBNL/ICSI, Traffic Lab at Ericsson Research in Hungary dataset) and a mixture of malicious and non-malicious dataset (ISCX 2012 (13/6/2010), ISCX 2012 (14/6/2010)). Figure 2.3 shows the schematic diagram of our proposed method that applies the Zipf's law to network traffic data for processing, analysis and malicious traffic detection.

2.7.7   Zipf's Law for Malicious, Non-malicious, Mixture of Malicious and Non-malicious Network Traffic

We investigate Zipf's law on the malicious, non-malicious and mixture of malicious and non-malicious network traffic data. Zipf's law plots and the corresponding P-value for each of the dataset are analysed. As a point of emphasis, we consider P-values > 0.1 to indicate that such a dataset fits the Power law (in this case Zipf's law), else the dataset fails to fit the power law.

From our experiments, Fig. 2.4 and Table 2.5 show that malicious dataset does not follow the Zipf's law when analysing the graphs and P-value.

We further show that the non-malicious dataset follows Zipf's law based on Zipf's law graphs and P-values as shown in Fig. 2.5 and Table 2.5.

Lastly, a mixture of malicious and non-malicious network traffic data does not follow Zipf's law based on the P-values obtained. Even though Zipf's law graph (Fig. 2.6) for the mixture of malicious and non-malicious datasets seem to follow Zipf's law, their P-values as shown in Table 2.5 do not follow Zipf's law.

This is an indication that naturally generated network traffic data follows Zipf's law. Whereas network traffic data that is malicious, deviates from this law.

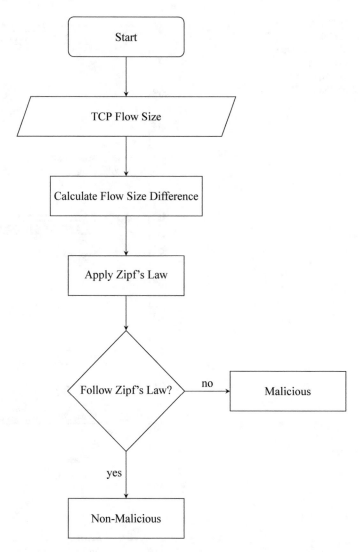

Fig. 2.3 Schematic diagram for our proposed method to differentiate malicious flows from non-malicious flows using Zipf's law

2.7.8 Comparative Analysis of Zipf's Law and Benford's Law with Implications

In this section, we compare Benford's law and Zipf's law based on our experimental results. Table 2.5 shows a comparison between Zipf's law P-values and Benford's law Chi-square divergence values with respect to the window sizes (w-size). For Zipf's law, we expect the P-values for the non-malicious datasets to be greater than 0.1

Fig. 2.4 Zipf's law for the malicious flow size difference of: **a** capture the hacker; **b** 2009 CDX dataset-35 dump; **c** 2009 CDX dataset-35 dump2

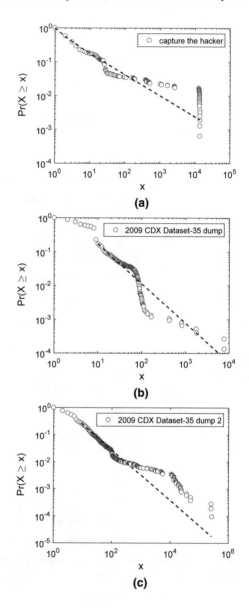

and those for the malicious datasets to be lower than 0.1. Based on our experimental Zipf's law results, we observe that the non-malicious datasets have P-values that are relatively larger as compared to the P-values obtained from the malicious dataset. However, for Benford's law, we expect the Chi-square divergence values for non-malicious dataset to be relatively smaller and the Chi-square divergence values for the malicious dataset to be relatively larger. We observe that Benford's law Chi-square divergence values obtained agree with the expected result.

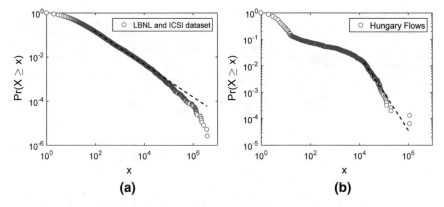

Fig. 2.5 Zipf's law for the non-malicious flow size difference of: **a** LBNL and ICSI dataset; **b** Traffic Lab at Ericsson Research in Hungary (TLERH) dataset

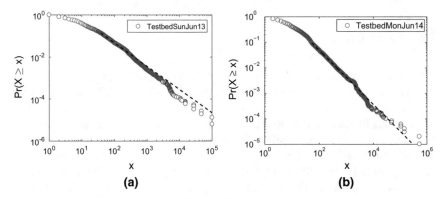

Fig. 2.6 Zipf's law for the mixture of malicious and non-malicious flow size difference of: **a** ISCX2012 (TestbedSunJun13) **b** ISCX2012 (TestbedSunJun14)

Based on our experimental results as shown in Table 2.5, the initial Zipf's law P-values obtained seem to be inversely proportional to Benford's law Chi-square divergence values. However, as only a few P-values are obtained, more results from other datasets would be needed before this assumption could be generalized. The implication of these results is that when Zipf's law and Benford's law are deployed in the same network environment to detect malicious traffic on the Internet, higher Zipf's law P-values and lower Benford's law Chi-square divergence values would be expected for normal network traffic. Conversely, when a malicious attack is taking place, the opposite conditions for both natural laws would occur, triggering an alert to the network administrator to perform a further investigation to determine the exact cause of the attack.

Table 2.5 Comparison between Zipf's law and Benford's law

Description	Quantity	Zipf's law P-value	w-size 2000	Benford's law divergence w-size 2000
Malicious (M)	HONEYBOT	0.0000	0.35986	–
	2009 CDX (dmp1)	0.0000	0.41638	–
	2009 CDX (dmp2)	0.0000	0.53069	–
Non-Malicious (N)	LBNL/ICSI	0.3080	0.06086	0.02335
	TLERH	0.1303	0.06206	0.04680
Mixture of N + M	ISCX 2012 (13/6/2010)	0.0000	0.37707	0.20355
	ISCX 2012 (14/6/2010)	0.0000	0.20078	0.10629

2.8 Conclusion

In this chapter, we applied and analysed Power laws (Benford's law and Zipf's law) to detect malicious traffic on the Internet. We showed that Benford's law and Zipf's law could be used effectively to detect whether a particular network was non-malicious or malicious by investigating its data using these laws. We showed that the average divergence values for non-malicious datasets were relatively low between the range of 0.003225103–0.089616951 as compared to malicious datasets with values between the range of 0.107162457–3.611008194. Moreover, Zipf's law P-values for non-malicious datasets were shown to follow Zipf's law, whereas Zipf's law P-values for malicious datasets did not follow this law. P-values of non-malicious datasets were 0.1303 and 0.3080 as compared to P-values of malicious datasets which were 0.0000 for all the datasets investigated. By comparing these two laws, we observed that the initial Zipf's law P-values obtained seem to be inversely proportional to Benford's law Chi-square divergence values. Therefore, these two laws are recommended for network traffic analysis in Nigeria. Hence, this will assist in curbing digitally facilitated crimes in Nigeria.

Acknowledgements The author would like to specially thank Prof. Anthony T.S. Ho, Prof. Adrian Waller, Prof. Shujun Li, Dr. Norman Poh and Dr. Santosh Tirunagari for their assistance.

References

1. Sambridge M, Tkalčić H, Jackson A (2010) Benford's law in the natural sciences. Geophys Res Lett 37(22)
2. Nigrini MJ, Mittermaier LJ (1997) The use of Benford's law as an aid in analytical procedures. Auditing 16(2):52

3. Mahanti A, Carlsson N, Arlitt M, Williamson C (2013) A tale of the tails: power-laws in Internet measurements. IEEE Netw 27(1):59–64
4. Arshadi L, Jahangir AH (2014) Benford's law behavior of internet traffic. J Netw Comput Appl 40:194–205
5. Faloutsos M, Faloutsos P, Faloutsos C (1999) On power-law relationships of the internet topology. In: ACM SIGCOMM Computer Communication Review, vol 29, pp 251–262. ACM
6. van Mierlo T, Hyatt D, Ching AT (2015) Mapping power law distributions in digital health social networks: methods, interpretations, and practical implications. J Med Internet Res 17(6)
7. Fu D, Shi YQ, Su Q (2007) A generalized Benford's law for JPEG coefficients and its applications in image forensics. In: Proceedings of the SPIE Multimedia Content Access: Algorithms and Systems
8. Li XH, Zhao YQ, Liao M, Shih FY (2012) Detection of tampered region for JPEG images by using mode-based first digit features. EURASIP J Adv Signal 1:1–10
9. Xu B, Wang J, Liu G, Dai Y (2011) Photorealistic computer graphics forensics based on leading digit law. J Electron (China) 28(1):95–100
10. Benford F (1938) The law of anomalous numbers. Proc Am Philos Soc 78:551–572
11. Pérez-González F, Heileman GL, Abdallah CT (2007) Benford's law in image processing. In: IEEE International Conference on Image Processing, vol 1, pp I–405. ICIP 2007 78:551–572. IEEE
12. Hill TP (1995) Base-invariance implies Benford's law. Proc Am Math Soc 123(3):887–895
13. Durtschi C, Hillison W, Pacini C (2004) The effective use of Benford's law to assist in detecting fraud in accounting data. J Forensic Account 5(1):17–34
14. Manning CD, Schtze H (1999) Foundations of statistical natural language processing. MIT Press
15. Newman MEJ (2005) Power laws, Pareto distributions and Zipf's law. Contemp Phys 46(5):323–351
16. Tao T (2009) Benford's law, Zipf's law, and the Pareto distribution. http://terrytao.wordpress.com/2009/07/03/benfords-law-zipfs-lawand-the-pareto-distribution/
17. Cristelli M, Batty M, Pietronero L (2012) There is more than a power law in Zipf. Sci Rep 2
18. Clauset A, Shalizi CR, Newman MEJ (2009) Power-law distributions in empirical data. SIAM Rev 51(4):661–703
19. Huang SH, Yen DC, Yang LW, Hua JS (2008) An investigation of Zipf's law for fraud detection. Decis Support Syst 46:70–83
20. Iorliam A, Ho ATS, Poh N, Tirunagari S, Bours P (2015) Data forensic techniques using Benford's law and Zipf's law for keystroke dynamics. In: 3rd International Workshop on Biometrics and Forensics (IWBF 2015). IEEE, pp 1–6
21. Kruegel C, Valeur F, Vigna G (2004) Intrusion detection and correlation: challenges and solutions, vol 14. Springer Science & Business Media
22. Sperotto A, Pras A (2011) Flow-based intrusion detection. In: IFIP/IEEE International Symposium on Integrated Network Management (IM), 2011. IEEE, pp 958–963
23. Patcha A, Park JM (2007) An overview of anomaly detection techniques: existing solutions and latest technological trends. Comput Netw 51(12):3448–3470
24. Gogoi P, Bhuyan MH, Bhattacharyya DK, Kalita JK (2012) Packet and ow based network intrusion dataset. In: Contemporary Computing, pp 322–334. Springer
25. Eskin E (2000) Anomaly detection over noisy data using learned probability distributions
26. Chan PK, Mahoney MV, Arshad MH (2003) A machine learning approach to anomaly detection. Department of Computer Sciences, Florida Institute of Technology, Melbourne
27. Simmross-Wattenberg F, Asensio-Perez JI, Casaseca de-la Higuera P, Martin-Fernandez M, Dimitriadis IA, Alberola-Lopez C (2011) Anomaly detection in network traffic based on statistical inference and alpha-stable modeling. IEEE Trans Dependable Secur Comput 8(4):494–509
28. Lu W, Ghorbani AA (2009) Network anomaly detection based on wavelet analysis. EURASIP J Adv Signal Process 2009:4
29. Bejtlich R (2004) The Tao of network security monitoring: beyond intrusion detection. Pearson Education

30. Steinberger J, Schehlmann L, Abt S, Baier H (2013) Anomaly detection and mitigation at internet scale: a survey. In: Emerging Management Mechanisms for the Future Internet, pp 49–60. Springer
31. Lakhina A, Papagiannaki K, Crovella M, Diot C, Kolaczyk ED, Taft N (2004) Structural analysis of network traffic flows, vol 32. ACM
32. Tune P, Roughan M (2013) Internet traffic matrices: a Primer. Recent Adv Netw. ACM SIG-COMM eBook, vol 1. ACM
33. Lawrence Berkeley National Laboratory and International Computer Science Institute (2005) LBNL/ICSI enterprise tracing project. http://www.icir.org/enterprise-tracing. Accessed 04 Apr 2015
34. Shiravi A, Shiravi H, Tavallaee M, Ghorbani AA (2012) Toward developing a systematic approach to generate benchmark datasets for intrusion detection. Comput Secur 31(3):357–374
35. Szabó G, Gódor I, Veres A, Malomsoky S, Molnár S (2010) Traffic classification over gbit speed with commodity hardware. IEEE J Commun Softw Syst 5
36. Pcap Traces (2015). http://www.simpleweb.org/wiki/Traces. Accessed 20 May 2015
37. NETRESEC AB. Publicly available PCAP files, http://www.netresec.com/?page=pcapfiles. Accessed 20 May 2015
38. Inter-service academy cyber defense competition (2009). https://www.itoc.usma.edu/research/dataset/. Accessed 20 May 2015
39. Capture files from Mid-Atlantic CCDC (2015). http://www.netresec.com/?page=MACCDC. Accessed 20 May 2015
40. Sperotto A, Sadre R, van Vliet DF, Pras A (2009) A labeled data set for ow-based intrusion detection. In: Proceedings of the 9th IEEE International Workshop on IP Operations and Management, IPOM 2009, Venice, Italy. Lecture Notes in Computer Science, vol 5843. Springer, pp 39–50
41. Song J, Takakura H, Okabe Y (2008) Cooperation of intelligent honeypots to detect unknown malicious codes. In WOMBAT Workshop on Information Security Threats Data Collection and Sharing. WISTDCS'08., pp 31–39. IEEE
42. Saad S, Traore I, Ghorbani A, Sayed B, Zhao D, Lu W, Felix J, Hakimian P (2011) Detecting P2P botnets through network behavior analysis and machine learning. In: Proceedings of 2011 9th Annual International Conference on Privacy, Security and Trust (PST 2011), pp 174–180. IEEE

Chapter 3
Combination of Natural Laws (Benford's Law and Zipf's Law) for Fake News Detection

Abstract With the increase in the number of character assassination and fake news recently happening in Nigeria, we combine Zipf's law and Benford's law to analyse and detect fake news. The problem of fake news has become one of the most prominent issues in Nigeria recently. In this chapter, the challenges fake news poses to Nigeria is briefly presented. Due to these challenges, we propose the combination of Benford's law and Zipf's law in news analysis such that the hybrid of the two laws will obey the Power law for real news and deviate for fake news. We carried out various tests on different real news sources and the result shows that real news obeys the Power law. We, therefore, propose that fake news should not obey the Power law even though we could not test on fake news sources because of the lack of verified fake news dataset.

Keywords Fake news · Benford's law · Zipf's law

Fake news is simply defined as 'a news article that is intentionally and verifiably false [1]'. Fake news is actually difficult to differentiate from real/authentic news. It is even more worrisome that people easily read and click on fake news links because they want to be up to date with the current happenings around them, have a sense of urgency, have sociopolitical polarization and due to curiosity or fear [2]. It is shocking to note that cyber criminals can use fake news as a bait to get their victims to perform their fraudulent activities. For example, clicking on a fake news link could lead to giving hackers access to your digital devices (e.g. computers and phones). This could lead to the cyber criminals accessing victims password, personal information, financial information capable of defrauding the victim of their funds. Once a victim clicks on such fake news, it could an infected news, it could infect not only their system but also the entire company's network [2].

In Nigeria, fake news is a great challenge. This has created much fear and warnings from Nigerian scholars, information experts and Nigerian government. A case in hand is the warning from Nobel Laureate, Prof. Wole Soyinka, who stated that 'Nigeria may start a World War III through fake news [3]'. If care is not taken fake news will lead to a cyber war within a country or even one country fighting with another country. Joseph Carson, an experienced enterprise security expert stated that: 'Only one fake news story from a trustworthy source can devalue an entire news feed [4]'.

© The Author(s), under exclusive license to Springer Nature Switzerland AG 2019   23
A. Iorliam, *Cybersecurity in Nigeria*, SpringerBriefs in Cybersecurity,
https://doi.org/10.1007/978-3-030-15210-9_3

Fake news has been rampant on social media, and news outlet. The news (later confirmed fake news) that made Nigerians worrisome was the fact that some news outlets stated that they were very sure the Nigerian President (President Mohammadu Buhari) was confirmed dead in London. After some time, the president returned to Nigeria [5]. To emphasize how scary fake news is in Nigeria, even the INEC are worried about the negative effects fake news could have in the 2019 elections and the Nigerian democracy. As such, their staff were recently trained to detect and uncover fake news [6].

This means there is every need to detect and classify fake news from real/authentic news. One of the most suitable techniques in differentiating fake news from authentic news should have been supervised learning. Unfortunately, using supervised learning means that there should be clear labels showing what is fake news and what is real/authentic news. For the fact that the above task seems difficult currently, then supervised learning cannot effectively detect/classify fake news. Again, there are no publicly available labelled fake news databases for experiments. The most closely related tool that has been able to generate pseudo fake reviews is the Amazon Mechanical Turk (ATM) crowd sourcing tool. But it should be noted that ATM generates reviews that cannot be totally considered as fake. It is in a way unnatural, as such this kind of data is not suitable for experiments that relate to detecting/classifying fake news from authentic news especially with Natural laws (such as Benford's law and Zipf's law).

In Nigeria, fake news and hate speech are classified to be similar to each other. Nigerians are warned that before sharing information on Facebook, Twitter, Instagram or WhatsApp, two things should be considered such as 'how credible is the source' and 'share what you can only vouch for'. Nigeria is doing its best to curb fake news. Recently, CrossCheck Nigeria was launched to check and detect potential fake news. This is launched in Nigeria by a UK-based investigative journalism outfit, International Centre for Investigative Reporting (ICIR) and First Draft News [7]. Even though such platforms have started coming up in Nigeria to curb fake news, the rate of fake news on social media and other news outlets is increasing tremendously. As such, there is every need to develop more effective tools/techniques to curb this serious challenge.

3.1 Combination of Benford's Law and Zipf's Law for Fake News Detection

In most cases what appears to be fake news may just use exaggeration and introduce some non-factual elements, and is intended to amuse or make a point, rather than to deceive. Therefore, it is very tricky for detecting fake news. However, we propose a novel method designed to analyse different news sources and detect fake news. The aim of this study is to analyse and differentiate between real news and fake news data set using the hybrid of Benford's and Zipf's law. Benford's law and Zipf's law are carefully explained in Sect. 3.2. Briefly, a review of the most relevant research on Benford's law and Zipf's law is presented. Tirunagari et al. [8], presented a method for differentiating Alzheimer's disease (AD) patients from healthy ones based on their electroencephalograms (EEG) signals using Benford's law and support vector machines (SVMs) with a radial basis function (RBF) kernel. They divided EEG signals from 11 AD and 11 age-matched controls into artefact-free 5-sec epochs and trained the SVM. They performed tenfold cross-validation at both the epoch- and subject-level to evaluate the importance of each electrode in discriminating between AD and healthy subjects. In their research, they found that performance across the electrodes was reduced when subject-level cross-validation was performed, but relative performance across the electrodes was found to be consistent using epoch-level cross validation. Iorliam et al. [9] used the divergence values of Benford's law as input features for a Neural Network for the classification and source identification of biometric images. Their experimental analysis shows that the classification and identification of the source of the biometric images can achieve good accuracies between the range of 90.02 and 100%. Iorliam et al. [10] in their investigation to examine whether biometric images will follow Benford's law and whether or not they can be used to detect potential malicious tampering of biometric images discovered that, the biometric samples do indeed follow Benford's law; and the method can detect tampering effectively, with Equal Error Rate (EER) of 0.55% for single-compressed face images, 2.7% for single-compressed fingerprint images, 4.3% for double-compressed face images and 3.7% for double-compressed fingerprint images. Iorliam et al. [11] in their paper, investigated the use of keystroke data to distinguish between humans using keystroke biometric systems and non-humans for auditing application. The authors noted that Benford's Law and Zipf's Law, which are both discrete Power law probability distributions, have been effectively used to detect fraud and discriminate between genuine data and fake/tampered data. As such, their motivation was to apply Benford's Law and Zipf's Law on keystroke data and to determine whether they follow these laws and discriminate between humans using keystroke biometric systems from non-humans. From their results, it is observed that, the latency values of the keystroke data from humans actually follow Benford's law and Zipf's law, but not the duration values. There are a number of unsolved issues concerning the analysis of the fake news and propaganda especially in Nigeria. In this research, we will analyse news sources as a dataset using Benford's and Zipf's law. Iorliam [12] stated that combining Benford's law and Zipf's should improve the performance of differentiating authentic data from fake data. Hence, we are motivated from [12] to combine these two laws for fake news detection.

The main steps to combine Benford's law and Zipf's law for fake news detection are as follows:

1. Load the news to be investigated into the developed system.
2. Analyse the data using Benford's law and Zipf's law.
3. Combine the results for Benford's law and Zipf's law.
   Note: The data analysed by Benford's law are fused to be classified as Ranks and Frequencies. As such, both the values for Benford's law and Zipf's law are

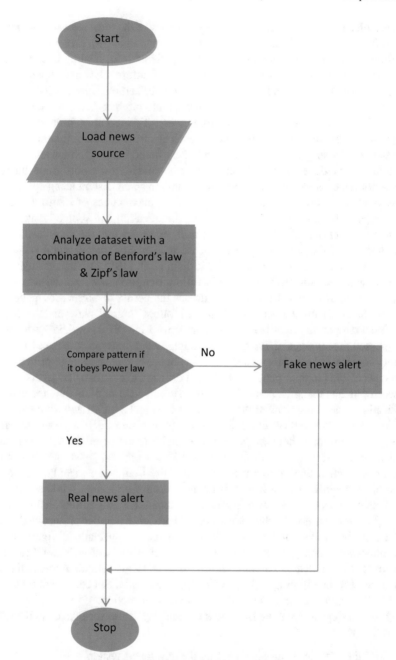

Fig. 3.1 A Combined Benford's and Zipf's law for fake news detection flowchart

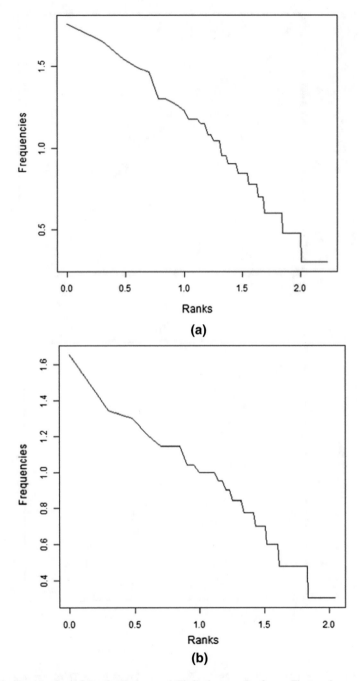

Fig. 3.2 Combination of Benford's law and Zipf's law results for: **a** First real news dataset; **b** Second real news datasets

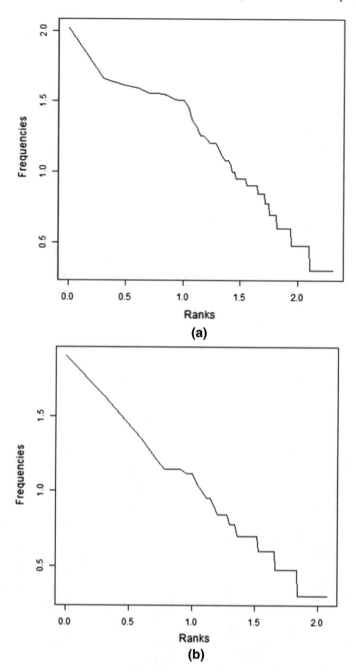

Fig. 3.3 Combination of Benford's law and Zipf's law results for: **a** Third real news dataset; **b** Fourth real news datasets

now in Ranks and Frequencies. In this way, alphanumeric dataset could also be analysed.

4. Plot the $log_{10}(R)$ against $log_{10}(F)$ for values obtained in (3).
5. Analyse the patterns and identify irregularities.
6. Patterns that follow Power laws should be real/authentic news whereas patterns that deviate from Power law should be fake/fabricated news.

Figure 3.1 shows the flowchart of the proposed system. The proposed system is designed to analyse news with the combination of Benford's law and Zipf's law. Furthermore, compare its patterns against the Power law. All patterns that deviate from the Power law are supposed to be fake news.

3.2 Results and Discussions

Based on the proposed method in Sect. 3.1, four news datasets believed to be real/authentic are plotted to observe their patterns as shown in shown in Figs. 3.2 and 3.3. It should be noted that these datasets are randomly picked. This means that properly labeled dataset should be investigated for this proposed method. This labeled dataset should be for real/authentic news and fake/fabricated news and should be publicly available so that other scientists could repeat these experiments and achieve similar results. From Figs. 3.2 and 3.3, it is observed the resultant plots produces a pattern that obeys the Power law. This shows that real news follows the Power law. However, more analysis should be done and the patterns observed for the cases of real/authentic dataset compared against fake/fabricated dataset. Furthermore, the P-Values for each of the cases should be calculated and compared under the hypothesis that P-values for the real news datasets should be greater than 0.1 and those for the fake news/fabricated news should to be lower than 0.1.

3.3 Conclusion

In this chapter, we combined Benford's law and Zipf's law to perform analysis such that the hybrid of the two laws will obey a Power law for real news dataset and a deviation for fake news dataset. The prevalent rate of fake news and propaganda is on the rise and there are really not much research work going on to combat fake news in Nigeria. The use of a combination of Benford's law and Zipf's law in news analysis has proven that all real news sources obeys the Power law. We, however, proposed that fake news sources will behave differently, i.e. not obeying the Power law. During this research work, we were able to get verified real news sources for analysis but we could not get verified or certified fake news sources, hence we are proposing that the analysis of fake news sources will behave differently.

In our future work, we plan to do the following:

   i. Perform experiments on realistic fake news
   ii. Compare the experiments in (i) with that of the realistic real news.

More results from other real news and fake news datasets would be needed before this assumption could be generalized.

Acknowledgements The author would like to specially thank Mr. William Waakaa and Mr. Myom Atu for their assistance. Furthermore, the author expresses huge thanks to Prof. Anthony T. S. Ho for his support.

References

1. Shu K, Sliva A, Wang S, Tang T, Liu H (2017) Fake news detection on social media: a data mining perspective. ACM SIGKDD Explor Newsl 19(1):22–36
2. New England College. How fake news leads to cyber attacks. https://www. newenglandcollegeonline.com/resources/communications/how-fake-news-leads-to-cyber-attacks/2019. Accessed 19 Jan 2019
3. New England College (2019) #BeyondFakeNews: Nigerian may start World War III through fake news Soyinka. https://www.vanguardngr.com/2019/01/beyondfakenews-nigerian-may-start-world-war-iii-through-fake-news/. Accessed 19 Jan 2019
4. Carson J (2019) Will fake news lead to the next cyber war? https://thycotic.com/company/blog/2018/03/16/fake-news-disruption-and-cyber-war/. Accessed 19 Jan 2019
5. techcabal.com (2018) Nigeria has a fake news problem its not paying attention to. https://techcabal.com/2018/08/03/nigeria-has-a-fake-news-problem-its-not-paying-attention-to/. Accessed 19 Jan 2019
6. guardian.ng (2019) Election: INEC trains staff to detect, counter fake news. https://guardian.ng/news/election-inec-trains-staff-to-detect-counter-fake-news/. Accessed 19 Jan 2019
7. premiumtimesng.com (2019) Platform to check fake news launched in Nigeria. https://www.premiumtimesng.com/news/top-news/298087-platform-to-check-fake-news-launched-in-nigeria.html. Accessed 19 Jan 2019
8. Tirunagari S, Abasolo DE, Iorliam A, Ho AT, Poh N (2017) Using benfords law to detect anomalies in electroencephalogram: an application to detecting alzheimers disease. In: 2017 proceedings on IEEE CIBCB, 21 Dec 2017
9. Iorliam A, Ho ATS, Waller A, Zhao X (2016) Divergence using benfords law, networks neural, for classification and source identification of biometric images. In: Shi Y, Kim H, Perez-Gonzalez F, Liu F (eds) Digital forensics and watermarking, IWDW (2016), Lecture Notes in Computer Science, vol 10082. Springer, Cham
10. Iorliam A, Ho ATS, Poh N, Shi YQ (2014) Do biometric images follow Benford's law? In: 2014 international workshop on biometrics and forensics (IWBF)
11. Iorliam A, Ho ATS, Poh N, Tirunari S, Bours P (2015) Data forensic techniques using Benfords law and Zipfs law for keystroke dynamics. In: Conference on international workshop on biometrics and forensics (IWBF 2015), Gjøvik, Norway
12. Iorliam A (2016) Application of power laws to biometrics, forensics and network traffic analysis. Doctoral dissertation, University of Surrey

Chapter 4
Cybersecurity and Mobile Device Forensic

Abstract Issues relating to cybersecurity and its challenges in Nigeria can be traced as far back as the provision of Internet services to Nigerians in 1996. Nigerians are known for the huge frauds they commit using the Internet. This chapter treats cybersecurity challenges/conflicts history in Nigeria. Furthermore, it looks at the relevant laws guiding against cyber crimes in Nigeria. Lastly, the need for embracing cybersecurity and mobile device forensics is encouraged.

Keywords Cybersecurity · Mobile device · Internet fraud

Cybersecurity can be defined as the protection and preservation of confidentiality, integrity and availability (CIA) of information which is in asset, in the realm of cyber space [1]. In essence, the CIA is specifically modelled as a guide for any company, organization or country with respect to security issues.

By confidentiality, security experts are concerned with controlling access to sensitive information. This is concerned with giving of access to information to the right persons and also making sure the wrong people do not have access to these sensitive information. This means such information should never be modified by unauthorized persons. This ensures that personal privacy and proprietary information is protected.

When a company, organization or country is concerned with how accurate and trustworthy information is, then it is referred to as integrity. Whether data is stationary or in transit, such data should be consistent, accurate and trustworthy at all times. In essence, integrity ensures non-repudiation, accuracy and authenticity of information.

Furthermore, when there is a guarantee for reliable and timely access to sensitive data for the right/authorized persons in an organization, company or country, this is referred to as availability.

In Nigeria, confidentiality of financial information and personal health care cannot be guaranteed. As such, cyber criminals take advantage of these weaknesses that could be a result of network design, software, communication channel and people to commit crimes for financial gains or victimization. As such, information on the Nigerian cyber space needs to be highly confidential to avoid such cases.

Furthermore, Nigeria needs to ensure that data integrity and system integrity are in place if we really want to fight and win the cyber warfare and its criminals. By data integrity we mean, information and programs should be changed only for specified and authorized cases. Considering system information, we mean such a system 'performs its intended function in an unimpaired manner, free from deliberate or inadvertent unauthorized manipulation of the system [2]'.

Lastly, in Nigeria, sensitive systems and data are intentionally or unintentionally available to unauthorized persons. It is worth noting that it becomes very scary when sensitive data is not accessible when needed by authorized persons. In the above interpretation of the CIA it is very clear that, the Nigerian cyber space and the interconnected digital devices must be operated in conformity with the CIA model before cyber crimes could be a curb in Nigeria.

The above definition and interpretation of cybersecurity dwells on the CIA model. The term cybersecurity could also be considered as the body of rules put in place for the protection of cyber space. By cyber space, we mean the notional environment in which communication over computer network occurs.

Even though cybersecurity is targeted at securing the cyber space, attackers keep evolving with new techniques to carry out their fraudulent activities on the cyber space. These cyber crimes have caused so many challenges in Nigeria and abroad, as such Nigerians and foreigners are not convinced about Internet transactions and computer-related operations especially when they involve financial transactions. Furthermore, it is even a greater concern that the Nigerian digital ecosystem is interwoven with the foreign cyber space. Due to these cyber crimes, foreigners are worried while transacting Internet business with Nigerians.

It is an established fact that the Internet has presented huge benefits to Nigerians to perform important positive tasks, however, fraudsters have turned the Internet into performing their fraudulent activities, and as such causing different harms to individuals residing within Nigeria and outside of the country. We can confidently put that the usage of the Internet in Nigeria is both a blessing and a curse. The use of computers and networks for fraud, financial embezzlement, theft, forgery, etc. is a very common practice in Nigeria. More concerns have increased recently on transactions involving the Nigerian cyber space and digital devices. This is because there is a tremendous increase in the rate at which digital devices (e.g. phones, computers, PDAs) are connected to the Internet in Nigeria recently. Even though transactions such as Internet banking, purchase of top-up cards, are conveniently done at homes, attackers also take advantage of this and use these devices to commit different frauds as well. This is a great concern and it needs to be urgently addressed to save the image of Nigeria and to make the Nigerian digital ecosystem free from such frauds.

4.1   Nigeria and Internet Fraud

In 2017, the Nigerian Communication Commission (NCC) stated that Nigeria ranks third globally when considering cyber crimes. Furthermore, the Director General of NCC, Prof. Umar Danbatta stated that Nigeria is rated the most Internet fraudulent country in Africa [3]. As the rate of cyber fraud in Nigeria is very high, the number

Table 4.1 Internet users, country population data and percentage of population that use Internet in 2017 [4]

Country	Internet users	Country population	Percentage of population that use the internet (%)
United States	312.23 million	325.7 million [5]	~96
United Kingdom	63.06 million	66.02 million [5]	~96
Nigeria	98.39 million	190.9 million [5]	~50

of Internet users are only ~50% of the entire population of Nigeria as can be seen in Table 4.1 [4]. This is really scary because if the nothing is done in curbing these cyber crimes, as the percentage of Internet users increase, we should expect a proportional increase in the rate of cyber crimes.

Based on this alarming observation, in recent years the law enforcement agencies such as the Economic and Financial Crime Commission (EFCC), Independent Corrupt Practice and other related offences Commission (ICPC), State Security Service (SSS), the Nigeria Police (particularly the Force Criminal Investigation Department (FCID)) among others have been playing prominent roles in fighting against the new trend of social vices. These bodies responsible for fighting against crimes in Nigeria are explained below:

- EFCC: The EFCC was established in 2003 and it is a Nigerian law enforcement agency, investigating financial crimes such as Advance Fee Fraud (419) and money laundering. Many people have accused the EFCC of being a government agency to hurt people that are on the political opposition side. Most people feel, the EFCC beamed its searchlight on political foes of a President. Furthermore, there exists huge criticism in the way in which even when money and other items are recovered from fraudulent individuals, there is no proper account of how the money and items were used. The EFCC head (Chairman) has been greatly criticized over the years for being manipulated by the Government in power. Developing a software that would monitor Internet services in the country as a way to combat cyber crime will assist the EFCC in gathering the required evidence to acquit or convict a person under their investigation.
- ICPC: It was inaugurated on 29 September 2000 and their mandate is to receive and investigate reports of corruption and in appropriate cases prosecute the offender(s). The ICPC targets corruption in the public sector, especially bribery, gratification and abuse and misuse of office.
- SSS: It is also referred to as the Department of State Services (DSS) and is the primary domestic intelligence agency in Nigeria. It was formed in 1986 and is mainly concerned with gathering of intelligent information within the country and for the protection of senior government officials, particularly the President and Governors.
- Nigeria Police (Force Criminal Investigation Department): The Nigeria Police Force is designated by Section 194 of the 1979 constitution and was formed in 1930, whose main duty is to fight crimes. Departments under the Nigeria Police

Force include the Force Criminal Investigation Department (FCID), which is the highest investigative arm of the Nigeria Police Force. Its primary functions include investigation and prosecution of serious and complex criminal cases within and outside the country.

Due to the fact that these law enforcement agencies are doing their best to fight against cyber crimes, a preventive measure which can be considered by these agencies is closely linked to providing digital surveillance to prevent digital crimes in the Nigerian cyber space. It is scary to note that evidence on digital devices are intentionally or unintentionally deleted in Nigeria and as such making investigations quite hard. For example, the Internet browsing history and log files from fraudulent Internet conversations and computer history can easily be overwritten in most cases. Thus erasing substantial and tangible evidence of fraudulent conversations or acts been carried out by a particular person or group of persons while communicating. The lack of evidence in many instances has inspired a better approach in which conversations can be captured using automated capturing approaches, which can serve as evidence to support or refute allegation in the court of law. Evidence captured by a computer or other devices, if not tampered with can be admissible in the court of law both in the UK and Nigeria. According to Bainbridge [6], evidence that is automatically recorded by a computer or other device or machine without further human intervention, is referred to as real evidence and is generally admissible in the UK court. Examples of such evidence include images recorded by CCTV, and the time and date stamp on an email. This is not an exception in Nigeria; as Section 84 of the Evidence Act 2011 provides that a statement contained in a document produced via a computer, which is relevant to the facts in issue is admissible as evidence in the court. Section 258(1) (d) of the Act further describes a document for the purpose of legal alert to include 'any device by means of which information is recorded, stored or retrievable including computer output' [7]. The above statement clearly shows that captured evidence from automated software if not tampered with, will be admissible in the court of law both in the UK and Nigeria. In order to prove that the evidence is not tampered with, a hash value of the evidence is very important to show that the evidence has not changed before and after the analysis [8].

4.2   Reasons for Increase in Cyber Crimes in Nigeria

There are so many reasons why Nigerians engage in cyber crimes. Below are some of the reasons:

1. Increase in Unemployment Rate: It is an established fact that Nigerians are well known for acquiring education and skills. Unfortunately, after acquiring these education and skills there are no jobs available for them. For example, in 2018, the unemployment rate in Nigeria was about 23.10% [9]. When these skilled graduates are not employed, they tend to use the Internet to commit cyber crimes.

2. Desperation to Make Wealth: The distribution of wealth in Nigeria does not follow a Pareto distribution (80–20 law). The gap between the rich and the poor is really wide. Most youths due to extreme poverty and no availability of legal means to make wealth tend to cyber crimes to become rich overnight. Hence, one of the reasons for increase in cyber crimes in Nigeria.

3. Lack/Enforcement of Cyber Crime Laws: Nigeria as a country has cyber crime laws as discussed in Sect. 4.5. However, they do not properly address all the cyber crimes that are carried out by Nigerians within the country and abroad. Surprisingly, even the established cyber crime laws in Nigeria are not properly enforced to track down offenders. As such cyber criminals most times go unpunished.

4. Lack of Forensics/Security Experts: Even though there are a lot of crimes that are committed using the Internet and digital devices in Nigeria, we have very few forensics/security experts. Even the few forensic/security experts that are available in nigeria are underutilized in combating these cyber crimes. Furthermore, lack of forensic laboratories/tools in Nigeria is greatly hampering the fight against cyber criminals.

5. Negative Role Models: It is shocking to admit that Nigeria is a country where ill gotten wealth is celebrated. Therefore, the younger generation has learnt this unfortunate act. This has led to most youths indulging in cyber crimes in order to become wealthy so that they could also be celebrated.

6. Urbanization: There is a huge difference between people living in rural areas from the ones staying the urban areas. This is because the people living in rural areas lack basic amenities such as electricity, healthcare facilities, Internet services, etc. As such, rural people move to urban areas to settle for greener pastures. As they get to these urban areas, it gets tougher for them to survive. As such, the quickest way to make a living is by indulging in cyber crimes and related crimes for survival. However, if basic amenities are provided in rural areas, there will be no need for urbanization in most cases. Furthermore, even the rural people that migrate to towns, if basic amenities are provided by the government to carter for its urban citizens then there will be less cyber crimes.

4.3   Types of Cyber Crimes in Nigeria

It is a very difficult task to solve cyber crimes due to the fact that it takes different forms. This section explains some of the most prevalent cyber crimes that are practiced in Nigeria.

1. Fraud-Identity Theft: Online identity theft is very common in Nigeria. This is usually targeted for financial gains (financial identity theft). They steal personal information especially financial account details by either providing a link that takes an innocent user (a target) to a particular form or creating a false bank website or organization website (cloning). Once the form is filled by the target, all the needed financial account details are captured and could be used to defraud

the target. This defrauding could be aimed at stealing the targets funds or transferring the targets funds to a different account (especially a foreign account) to be used later. This could also be referred to as phishing, which is typically achieved by email spoofing. Usually, cyber criminals use social engineering approaches to trick their target on clicking a particular link. Once this is done, they could carry out their fraudulent activities instantly or periodically, depending on what they intend to do.

Recently, the bank verification number (BVN) scams have increased in Nigeria. This was an initiative of the central bank of Nigeria (CBN) to link an 11-digit number to all individuals that have an account with different banks in Nigeria. Even though this initiative was targeted at reducing fraudulent activities of individuals having huge sums in accounts that could not be traced, it rather paved way for cyber criminals to carry out their fraudulent activities. Cyber criminals usually send out text messages or make calls to their target demanding their BVNs. Once they get hold of this BVNs, they use it maliciously to defraud their target.

2. Hacking: Even though ethical hackers are important for testing system vulnerabilities and accessing computers without permission, in Nigeria cyber criminals use it for fraudulent purposes. Such fraudulent activities are motivated from love for money, fame, power and show-off of their expertise amongst several other reasons.

3. Cyber terrorism: Terrorism in Nigeria has increased tremendously recently. Boko Haram activities in Nigeria are getting out of control as each day passes by. Most shockingly, the terrorist use the cyber space to upload videos aimed at carrying out their threats against the Nigerian government and individuals. These cyber terrorists request for ransoms from government and individuals of interest. As such, they are making life very uncomfortable for Nigerian citizens and even foreigners.

4. Web Jacking: This attack is aimed at taking control of a government or an organization website fraudulently. This is aimed at changing the content of the website for fraudulent activities or re-directing a target to a different but similar website to collect relevant information from their target. The attacker then asks for ransoms from the organizations that their websites are hijacked. They may aim at defrauding also the people that visit such websites especially if such websites collect financial payments. This is similar to phishing but it is not really phishing in the sense that when the mouse is hovered over the original company website, the URL is original. The attacker executes his/her plan only when you click a new link that they provide. As such, it takes you to a slightly different website and this is where they defraud their victim.

5. Cyber stalking: It has become a very common practice by cyber criminals in Nigeria to follow or pursue people online. This is technically looked at as an invasion of one's privacy online. Pedophiles stalk little children and some men stalk ladies using the Internet. In Nigeria, the usage of Facebook and other related social media has increased. However, issues around cyber stalking (either Internet or computer stalking) are not even considered by individuals as crimes.

There is every need to curb these crimes in the Nigerian cyber space to make it very safe for usage.

6. Ransomware: Skilled attackers in Nigeria navigate into organization or company's computer network to encrypt their important files. They demand for huge ransoms from their target to grant them access to the encrypted files.
7. Software Piracy: In Nigeria, it has become very common that software is pirated on a daily basis. As such, intellectual properties are not valued in Nigeria.

From the above explanation of cyber crimes that happen in Nigeria, it is better we think like cyber criminals and get a step ahead of them to solve cyber crimes in Nigeria.

4.4   Link Between Mobile Device Forensics and Cybersecurity

Mobile device forensics deals with the recovery of evidence from mobile devices in a forensically sound manner with forensic methods [10, 11]. These mobile devices include mobile phones, PDAs, tablet computers, GPS devices and the general internal structure of these devices such as their SIM cards and phone memory. Recently, almost all mobile devices are connected to the Internet. As such, securing only the cyber space without securing mobile devices that connect to the Internet would just be a waste of time and energy. To investigate mobile devices in Nigeria is quite a difficult task. This is because different types of mobile devices are under circulation in Nigeria. Therefore, a mobile device forensic expert needs to be very skilled before they can effectively perform investigations on such devices. Having a very good understanding of computer forensics and how its tools work is not enough to be an expert in mobile device forensics. For example, desktop systems could mostly fall within the MS Windows, OS X from Apple Inc., and Linux. However, for mobile devices, the OS market ranges from Android OS, Apple iOS, Blackberry, Symbian and Microsoft. Surprisingly, in most cases, the storage of data and access rights on most of these OSs are different. Nigeria has phones that are manufactured from around the world including China. The interesting thing about these phones is that the outward appearances of these phones may look like a different model (e.g. Nokia) but the OS may be different. As such mobile device forensics in Nigeria is a difficult task and needs to be done by skilled experts. Mobile device forensic experts are faced with the challenge to extract data using physical or logical approaches. It is challenging because extracting data at the physical level gives a mobile device forensic expert the entire content of the phone, as such it is time consuming, requires complex and expensive equipment as well. Moreover, the data obtained at this level is raw and in most cases encrypted. Even if such data could be decrypted, only sophisticated mobile devices' forensic tools could be able to achieve such tasks. Strangely, if investigations involve a BlackBerry, for instance then accessing data at the physical level will not be possible. The challenge faced at accessing data at the logical level is that even though the accessed data can be in a human-readable form, the data acquired at this level is quite lower, as such, some sensitive information needed by a mobile device investigator may be missing. As such a mobile device forensic expert is placed in a dilemma as to whether to use the physical-level data extraction method or logical-level data extraction method for mobile device investigations.

To overcome the challenge presented by the logical method, Oxygen Software company in 2004 provided a method that installs an agent into the mobile device under investigation. As such, forensically important information such as logs, temporary files, cache, deleted data, etc. are available for a mobile device forensic expert for investigations. Processes such as device connection and data exchange are simplified by the agent provided by the Oxygen Software company. Table 4.2 clearly explains some of the top mobile device forensic tools and how they are utilized in solving mobile crimes. These tools are just for illustrative purposes as there are several other mobile device forensic tools that could aid mobile device forensic experts in performing their investigations.

Even though there lots of mobile device forensic tools to investigate mobile devices, there is every need to preserve evidence on such mobile devices. To achieve this, forensic investigators usually isolate such phones from a surrounding network. Extraction of evidence from mobile devices usually include [26]:

- Evidence Intake Phase: This stage is all about how requests for examinations are handled. This process involves request forms and the general paperwork to document everything about the phone under investigation. Information such as chain of custody, owner of the phone and the incident that occurred involving the phone etc are documented. The specific objectives for the examination of the phone under investigation is crucial to allow the investigator to decide what exactly to extract or do with cellular phones under investigation.
- Identification Phase: For examination to be successful, the examiner needs to identify clearly issues such as the following:

  - the legal authority to examine the phone,
  - goals of the examination,
  - make, model and identifying information for the cellular phone under investigation,
  - Removable and external storage,
  - any other source of potential evidence.

- Preparation: This involves proper research about the phone under investigation after the phone's make and model must have been identified. Such research involves the tools to use, the machines, equipment, cables, software and drivers needed for the successful examination of the phone under investigation.
- Isolation: For the fact that cellular phones can communicate with others through infrared, Bluetooth and wireless network capabilities, prior to any examination, such a phone is to be isolated from communicating with other devices. Isolation is very important to prevent addition or deletion of important information whether accidentally or intentionally.

Table 4.2 Top mobile device forensic tools and their descriptions

Mobile device forensic tools	Description
Cellebrite [12]	This is one of the best mobile device forensic tools for data extraction and analysis. It provides information such as device information (name, device type and version, serial number, phone number, Apple ID, accounts logged into, databases installed), call history (call logs, contact names and numbers, voicemail), gallery (photos or videos taken with the phone, including locations were taken), Internet activity (browsing and Internet search histories, including social media activity), text communications (SMS, MMS, iMessage, Facebook Messenger, WhatsApp, WeChat), and other important mobile phone evidence such as custom apps installed, music files, movies, downloaded data, wireless networks connected to the phone, etc. [13]
XACT/.XRY [14]	XACT mobile device forensic tool acquires physical data after a phone is seized from a suspect and allows mobile forensic experts to present such evidence to the court of law. Furthermore, the .XRY enables mobile device forensic experts to acquire the logical data from a seized phone under investigation [14]
Paraben device seizure [15]	This is a handheld forensic tool, which can access data at the physical and logical level. It has the capacity to recover deleted data, and full data dumps amongst several other things [15]. Basically, it is an acquisition, examination and reporting tool that is used for Palm OS, Pocket PC and RIM OS phones. It supports only cable interface but does not support the recovery of SIM information
mobileforensicscentral.com [16, 17]	This website allows a mobile device investigator to carry out an initial review of the specifications of the mobile device under investigation. It is very useful when the kind of information to retrieve is not very clear but the mobile device forensic investigator needs to unravel it [16, 17]
BitPim [18]	This open-source software allows a mobile device investigator to view and manipulate data on many Code-Division Multiple Access (often found in the U.S and Russia) phones from LG, Samsung, Sanyo and other manufacturers [18]
Simcon [19]	It securely images the total files in a GSM SIM card for a mobile device forensic investigator to further analyse the contents of such SIM card. It has proved over the years to be the best when dealing with the analysis of a SIM card under investigation [19]
CellDEK [20]	This is a portable handset data extraction kit for use at the crime scene and all working environments associated with an investigation that is still ongoing. CellDEK has the capability to access, read and copy stored data from GSM, CDMA, TDMA, iDen handsets, SIM cards, PDAs and about 15 types of flash cards. The most interesting thing about this tool is that the integrity of data held on the device under investigation is maintained. It also has the capability to extract important information for mobile device forensic investigations such as the time and date, serial numbers (IMEI, IMSI), dialled calls, missed calls, received calls, phonebook (both handset and SIM), SMS (both handset and SIM), deleted SMS from SIM, calendar, memos and to do lists amongst other important information needed for investigation of such mobile devices [20]
pilot-link [21]	This is an acquisition tool that is used for Palm OS phones. It has the capability to support cable interface only. It is not properly termed as a forensic software but has the capability to acquire relevant information on Palm OS phones
Cell seizure [21]	This is an acquisition, examination and reporting tool that can be used for models such as the GSM, CDMA and TDMA phones. It has excellent capability in recovering information from internal and external SIM card and supports cable interface only
MOBILedit forensic [22]	This is an acquisition, examination and reporting tool that targets GSM/CDMA/PCS. It has the capability to perform investigations on the internal and external features of a SIM card. Furthermore, it can support the infrared and cable interfaces
TULP 2G [23]	This is an acquisition tool for GSM and CDMA phones. It has SIM card support (both internal and external), but requires PC/SC-compatible smart card reader when dealing with external SIM cards. Furthermore, it can support infrared, cable and Bluetooth interfaces
SIMIS [24]	This is an acquisition, examination and reporting tool. It is used for external SIM cards only
ForensicSIM [21]	This is an acquisition, examination and reporting tool. It is used for external SIM cards only. It has the capability to produce an exact physical copy of SIM for the prosecutor and defense to a set of data storage cards
Forensic card reader[25]	This is an acquisition and reporting tool. It is used for external SIM cards only

- Processing: This process involves extraction of the desired data from the phone after isolation.
- Verification: It is important to verify the accuracy of the data that is extracted from the phone.
- Documentation/Reporting: Contemporaneous notes should be used to document what happened throughout the process of investigating a phone. It should be noted that what is not documented did not happen.
- Presentation: A clear consideration should be given to how information extracted and documented will be presented to another investigator, prosecutor and to the court of law in a very clear, concise and simple way.
- Archiving: The extracted data and documentation from the cellular phone under investigation needs to be properly preserved. It is important to store data in a proprietary and non-proprietary format on standard and acceptable media formats. This is very important in cases, where repeatability of the investigation is needed to achieve similar results.

One major link/similarity between cybersecurity experts and mobile device forensics experts is that all of them are performing investigations with the aim of stopping crimes in order to protect people and assets. It is therefore very important for the Nigerian cyber space to be properly protected alongside the mobile devices that are connected to them. This will make sure that our cyber space is well protected against cyber criminals.

4.5   Cybersecurity Laws and Punishment in Nigeria

Nigeria as a country has laws guiding against cyber crimes. The most challenging issue is not just about the creation of more laws but the implementation of even the existing laws in Nigeria. Below is a description of some of the most relevant cyber crime laws in Nigeria and the punishment an offender gets for violating such laws.

1. Identity Theft or Identity Fraud: Cases of identity fraud has increased recently. For example, A Nigerian man (Adekunle Adetiloye) whose real name is Michael Adeyemo was convicted in the US and the AP news said he is the: 'mastermind behind a plot to steal the identities of 38,000 people and bilk dozens of banks out of millions of dollars' [27]. This Nigerian (Adekunle Adetiloye) breaks records for performing the largest credit card fraud scheme in US history [27]. Another Nigerian (Kevin Kunle Sodipo Williams) was jailed for six and half years in the US for stolen identity fraud scheme. This is not a good record to be attained by a Nigerian, hence the need to fight identity theft or identity fraud both within and outside Nigeria [28]. Furthermore, in Nigeria, there is general identity theft on social media and its a general concern to every Nigerian [29]. The above cases are just a few cases that Nigerians involve themselves with identity theft or identity fraud. This crime is punished under the Cybercrime Act and when a person is convicted of this crime, he/she will serve a 7-year jail term or a fine of N 5,000,000 or both.

2. Hacking (i.e. unauthorized access): In 2018, a suspected fraudster, Okoli Nmesoma connived with others to hack into a Nigerian bank (Ecobank) and defraud the bank of 207 million naira (~571239 USD) [30]. The Cybercrime Act, 2015 is established to take care of this kind of cases. The law prohibits, prevents, detects, prosecutes and punishes cyber crimes in Nigeria. This law ensures the protection of critical national infrastructure and also promotes cybersecurity and protects computer systems and networks, electronic communications, data and computer programs, intellectual property and privacy rights. As such this law applies throughout the Federal Republic of Nigeria. There are also appropriate penalties/punishments for violating the Cybercrime Act as found in [31].
3. Denial-of-Service Attacks: Nigeria has witnessed embarrassing denial of service attacks recently. For example, the Independent National Electoral Commission (INEC) admitted that its website was hacked and services on the website denied at the time of the attack [32]. Recently, the All Progressives Congress (APC) also claimed that its website was hacked and activities on the website denied by unidentified attackers [33]. This is scary and even though the Nigerian Cybercrime Act of 2015, Section 8 [31] addresses this challenge, getting the attackers and administering the prescribed punished has not been fully implemented.
4. Phishing: The popular 'Nigerian Prince Scam' is well known to a lot of people. The popular 419 fraud-first requests for some processing fee that will aid the target access some huge sums of money. Sometimes on dating websites, the scammers collect a targets financial details and defraud such a target. Sometimes, the old trick involves sending a message to a target claiming, they work in a bank and have discovered that one of the person's banking with them is dead and they are looking for a foreign person to assist them claim to such funds. Even though this scam is an old trick, the scammers are still using such trick and greedy people are still falling victim of this trick. Below is a sample of a recent message the attackers sent to a target:

Email Heading: urgent investment

Email Body:
As-Salamou Aleykoum.
I request your co-operation in my desire to find a foreign partner who will assist me in the relocation and investment of a deceased customer's abandoned fund in the bank where i work. i am his personal Accountant before his accidental death.
Furthermore, i would like to share this information with you in line with this inheritance fund (USD $19.3 Million Dollars) Nineteen Million Three Hundred Thousand US Dollars.
I am counting on your sense of confidentiality as it is my desire that you keep this business transaction secret to yourself.
Therefore if you are interested kindly get back to me without further delay for more details on how we could proceed.
AMINA OUADARAGOU My private Phone number and WhatsApp +226- 64-19-73-97

The scammers keep improving with the essence of defrauding their target, especially for financial gains. For example, in 2016, a 40-year-old man named 'Mike' compromised emails, as well as used romance scams to defraud his targets worth $60 m (£45 m). He was arrested in Portharcourt, Nigeria [34]. There is an improvement in the way the Nigerian 419 scams work. They use the Business Email Compromise (BEC) scams. BEC is defined 'as a sophisticated scam targeting businesses working with foreign suppliers and/or businesses that regularly perform wire transfer payments. The scam is carried out by compromising legitimate business e-mail accounts through social engineering or computer intrusion techniques to conduct unauthorized transfers of funds'. Between 2013 and May 2016, the BEC affected about 22,143 domestic and international victims with a total of $3,086,250,090 lost. It is shocking to note that the BEC is a direct evolution of the Nigerian 419 scam [35]. Under the Cybercrime Act, anyone that commits a phishing crime will be imprisoned for three years or a fine of N 1, 000, 000 or both.

5. Infection of IT Systems with Malware (e.g. Viruses, Trojans, Worms, Spyware, Ransomware): In 2017, a Nigerian man in his mid-20s residing in Nigeria was sending emails to his targets, claiming the emails were coming from 'Saudi Aramco' the world's second largest daily oil producer. The aim was to either use a phishing approach to steal financial details from his target or to trick his target to download a malware-infected attachment. He targeted more than 4000 companies and 14 were successful making him earn thousands of dollars in the process [36]. Under the Cybercrime Act, anyone that commits the above-described crime will be imprisoned for three years or a fine of N 1, 000, 000 or both.

6. Possession or use of hardware, software or other tools used to commit crimes (e.g. hacking tools) attracts imprisonment for not more than 2 years or a fine of not more than N 5,000, 000 or both.

7. Electronic theft crime attracts imprisonment for not more than 5 years or a fine of not more than N 7,000, 000 or both.

8. Activities that affect the security, confidentiality, integrity and availability of IT systems, infrastructures, communications network, device or data are properly punished by the law in Nigeria [37].

The above description emphasizes the fact that there exits laws to guide against cyber crimes, however, enforcing such laws with its punishment to offenders has not been implemented in Nigeria.

4.6 Conclusion

Nigeria has been known for Internet fraud. Even though there are several reasons why Nigerians involve in cyber crimes, this is an unacceptable act. Based on the fact that there is a link between mobile device forensics and cybersecurity, there is every need to encourage security experts to engage in these disciplines to assist in tackling cyber fraud in Nigeria.

References

1. Difenda (2018) What is the cia triangle and why is it important for cybersecurity management?, says NCC. https://www.difenda.com/blog/what-is-the-cia-triangle-and-why-is-it-important-for-cybersecurity-management. Accessed 11 Jan 2019
2. Houmb S H, Sallhammar K (2005) Modeling system integrity of a security critical system using colored petri nets. WIT Transactions on The Built Environment, 82. https://www.witpress.com/Secure/elibrary/papers/SAFE05/SAFE05001FU.pdf. Accessed 11 Jan 2019
3. Vanguard (2017) Nigeria 3rd in global internet crimes behind UK, US, says NCC. https://www.vanguardngr.com/2017/08/nigeria-3rd-global-internet-crimes-behind-uk-u-s-says-ncc/. Accessed 11 Jan 2019
4. The Statictica (2017) Countries with the highest number of internet users as of december 2017 (in millions). https://www.statista.com/statistics/262966/number-of-internet-users-in-selected-countries/. Accessed 11 Jan 2019
5. worldometers (2019) Current world population. http://www.worldometers.info/world-population/. Accessed 11 Jan 2019
6. Bainbridge D (2008) Introduction to information technology law. Longman, UK
7. Evidence Act (2011) Explanatory memorandum. http://resourcedat.com/wp-content/uploads/2012/01/Evidence_Act_2011.pdf. Accessed 11 Jan 2019
8. Iorliam A, James A (2013) Fraudulent activities using virtual meetings. Int J Comput Sci Eng 5(5):409
9. Trading economics (2019) Nigeria unemployment rate. https://tradingeconomics.com/nigeria/unemployment-rate. Accessed 12 Jan 2019
10. Farjamfar A, Abdullah MT, Mahmod R, Udzir NI (2014) A review on mobile devices digital forensic process models. Res J Appl Sci Eng Technol 8(3):358–66
11. Iorliam A (2018) Fundamental computing forensics for Africa: a case study of the science in Nigeria. Springer, Cham
12. cellebrite (n.d.). Digital intelligence for a safer world. https://www.cellebrite.com/en/home/. Accessed 12 Jan 2019
13. J. Bergerson (2017) Mobile phone forensics: understanding cellebrite extraction reports.https://www.iltanet.org/blogs/jason-bergerson/2017/03/17/mobile-phone-forensics-understanding-cellebrite-extraction-reports?ssopc=1. Accessed 24 Jan 2019
14. XACT. XACTMobile phone investigations go deeper. http://www.veille.ma/IMG/pdf/xact-datasheet.pdf. Accessed 24 Jan 2019
15. Paraben device seizure (2011) Android forensic techniques. https://www.sciencedirect.com/topics/computer-science/paraben-device-seizure. Accessed 24 Jan 2019
16. Pearson S, Watson R (2010) Digital triage forensics: processing the digital crime scene. Syngress, US
17. Mobile forensics central (2012). http://mobileforensicscentral.com/mfc/. Accessed 24 Jan 2019
18. bitpim (2010). http://www.bitpim.org/. Accessed 24 Jan 2019
19. SIMCon. SIM card acquisition and analysis with SIMCon. https://subscription.packtpub.com/book/networking_and_servers/9781785282058/1/ch01lvl1sec12/sim-card-acquisition-and-analysis-with-simcon. Accessed 24 Jan 2019
20. celldek (2007). https://www.officer.com/investigations/forensics/evidence-collection/product/10043165/forensic-science-service-celldek. Accessed 24 Jan 2019
21. Ayers AR, Jansen W, Delaitre AM, Moenner L (2007) Cell phone forensic tools: an overview and analysis update
22. mobiledit (2018). https://www.mobiledit.com/forensic-solutions/. Accessed 24 Jan 2019
23. Van Den Bos J, Van Der Knijff R (2005) TULP2Gan open source forensic software framework for acquiring and decoding data stored in electronic devices. Int J Digit Evid 4(2):1–9
24. SIMIS (2006). http://www.crownhillmobile.com/products.php. Accessed 24 Jan 2019
25. Forensic card reader (2013) http://www.avervision.com.tw/kiosk_avi-xm35.html. Accessed 24 Jan 2019

26. Murphy C (2011) cellular phone evidence data extraction and documentation
27. pulse.ng (2018) Nigerian man convicted of fraud on trial for stealing his own identity. https://www.pulse.ng/news/metro/nigerian-man-convicted-of-fraud-on-trial-for-stealing-his-own-identity/fpn6xpw. Accessed 12 Jan 2019
28. vanguardngr.com (2017) US court jails Nigerian over identity fraud. https://www.vanguardngr.com/2017/10/u-s-court-jails-nigerian-identity-fraud/. Accessed 12 Jan 2019
29. allafrica.com (2015). Nigeria: concerns over spate of identity theft on social media. https://allafrica.com/stories/201511092243.html. Accessed 17 Jan 2019
30. pmnewsnigeria (2019). Ecobank loses N207m to suspected fraudsters. https://www.pmnewsnigeria.com/2018/05/30/ecobank-loses-n207m-to-suspected-fraudsters/. Accessed 12 Jan 2019
31. Centre for laws of the federation of Nigeria (2015). Cybercrimes (Prohibition, Prevention, etc) act
32. vanguardngr.com. INEC website hacked. https://www.vanguardngr.com/2015/03/inec-website-hacked/. Accessed 17 Jan 2019
33. vanguardngr.com. APC website hacked. https://www.vanguardngr.com/2019/01/apc-website-hacked/. Accessed 17 Jan 2019
34. bbc.com. Online fraud: Top Nigerian scammer arrested. https://www.bbc.com/news/world-africa-36939751. Accessed 17 Jan 2019
35. Yedaly M, Wright B (2016) Cyber crime & cybersecurity trends in Africa. https://www.thehaguesecuritydelta.com/media/com_hsd/report/135/document/Cyber-security-trends-report-Africa-en.pdf
36. vanguardngr.com. Global hunt for Nigerian cyber criminal spreading malware. https://www.vanguardngr.com/2017/08/global-hunt-nigerian-cyber-criminal-spreading-malware/. Accessed 18 Jan 2019
37. iclg. Cybersecurity 2019 Nigeria. https://iclg.com/practice-areas/cybersecurity-laws-and-regulations/nigeria. Accessed 18 Jan 2019

Chapter 5
Proposed Digital Surveillance Software

Abstract The number of Nigeria's mobile subscribers reached 150 million users in 2017 [1]. For forensic experts and security experts, this is a great concern in terms of using the right security tools to investigate these devices when they are used for crime purposes. More strangely, most of the crimes that occur in Nigeria are performed on these digital devices and there is lack of evidence from these devices for admissibility in the court of law. Due to this challenge, a digital surveillance software (A-BOT) is proposed to secure Nigeria's cyber space and mobile devices from being used for cyber crimes and related crimes. Proper usage of A-BOT will serve as digital surveillance and prevent digital crimes in Nigeria.

Keywords Forensic · Digital surveillance · Cyber crime · A-BOT

5.1 Introduction

The law of evidence in Nigeria has made provision for the admissibility of computer-generated or electronic evidence in Nigeria through Section 84 of the Evidence Act 2011 [2]. Even though this law accepts computer evidence, it must fulfill certain conditions as stated below:

"(1) In any proceedings, statement contained in a document produced by a computer shall be admissible, as evidence of any fact stated in it, which direct oral evidence would be admissible, if it is shown that the conditions in subsection (2) of this section are satisfied in relation to the statement and computer in question".

This means admissibility of computer-generated evidence in the court of law can only be possible if subsection (2) below is met.

" (2) The conditions referred to in subsection (i) of this section are;

(a) that the documents containing the statement was produced by a computer during a period over which the computer was used regularly to store or process information for the purpose of any activities regularly carried on over that period, whether for profit or not, by anybody, whether corporate or not, or by any individual;

(b) that over that period, there was regularly supplied to the computer in the ordinary course of those activities information of the kind contained in the statement or of the kind contained in the statement of the kind from which the information so contained is derived;

(c) that throughout the material part of that period, the computer was operating properly or if not, that in any respect in which it was not operating properly, or was out of operation, during that part of that period, was not such as to affect the production of the document or the accuracy of its contents and

(d) that the information contained in the statement reproduces or is derived from information supplied to the computer in the ordinary course of those activities".

Furthermore, at any time there is a change of computer, or the computers are networked together, or the networked computers have been changed but the information gathered during this is serving as evidence, Section 3 handles these cases as shown below:

" (3) Where over a period, the function of storing or processing information for the purposes of any activities regularly carried on over that period as mentioned in subsection (2) of this section was regularly performed by computers, whether

(a) by a combination of computers operating over that period;

(b) by different computers operating in succession over that period

(c) by different combinations of computers operating in succession over that period; or

(d) in any other manner involving the successive operation over that period, in whatever order, of one or more computers and one or more computers and one or more computers and one or more combinations of computers, all the computers used for that purpose during that period shall be treated for the purposes of this section as constituting a single computer; and reference in this section to a computer shall be construed accordingly.

(4) In any proceeding where it is desired to give a statement in evidence by virtue of this section, a certificate.

(a) identifying the document containing the statement and describing the manner in which it was produced.

(b) giving such particulars of any device involved in the production of that document as may be appropriate for the purpose of showing that the document was produced by a computer;

(c) dealing with any of the matters to which the conditions mentioned in subsection (2) above relate, and purporting to be signed by a person occupying a responsible position in relation to the operation of the relevant device or the management of the relevant activities, as the same may be, shall be evidence of the matters stated in the certificate; and for the purposes of this subsection it shall be sufficient for a matter to be stated to the best of the knowledge and belief of the person stating it.

(5) For the purposes of this section.

(a) Information shall be taken to be supplied directly to a computer if it supplied to it any appropriate form and whether it is supplied directly (with or without human intervention) by means of any appropriate equipment;

(b) where, the course of activities carried on by any individual or body, information is supplied with a view to its being stored or processed for the purposes of activities by a computer operated otherwise than in the course of those activities, that information, if duly supplied to that computer, shall be taken to be supplied to it in the course of those activities;

(c) a document shall be taken to have been produced by a computer whether it was produced by it directly or (with or without human intervention) by means of any appropriate equipment".

Based on the above interpretations, digital evidence from mobile devices such as text messages, pictures, videos, call logs, etc. are potentially useful in many types of criminal investigation and court proceedings and are subject to be acceptable in the court of law if they adhere to the above description. Digital evidence have been an important component of the evidence presented in numerous high profile cases in recent years such as Dickson V Sylva and ORS (2016), Kubor V Dickson (2014), etc [3]. In most cases, the evidence concerned is often in form of short message service (SMS), instant messaging, call logs, etc. This research illustrates the potential for acquiring digital evidence data stored on mobile devices. Mobile devices are typically kept in close physical proximity to their owners as compared to other potential sources of digital evidence like computers. This enhances the potential value of digital evidence found on mobile devices of suspects, and the suspects may interact with them continuously throughout the day and may take them to the crime scene. In addition to traces of the suspect's communications, a suspect's phone may contain evidence pertaining to their location, and with the advent of the smartphone, they may contain the same rich variety of digital evidence which might be found on computer systems [4]. Mobile phones and their application may be involved in a large variety of criminal cases, including fraud, theft, money laundering, illicit distribution of copyrighted material or child pornographic images or even distribution of malware in cyber crime cases [4]. Even though mobile devices have very important information for forensic analysis and investigations, performing such investigations in a forensically sound manner is really a challenge [4].

As such, monitoring of cyber infrastructure in Nigeria has become imperative given that the rate of criminal activities has increased tremendously using technology. Cyber infrastructure consists of computing systems, data storage systems, advanced instruments and data repositories, visualization environments, and people, all linked by high-speed networks to make possible scholarly innovation and discoveries not otherwise possible. Information technology systems that provide particularly powerful and advanced capabilities could be referred to as cyber infrastructure [5]. The data used by organizations and government firms in Nigeria is considered as the oil of our digital economy [6]. When cyber infrastructures and the data they generate are not properly secured, terrorists/attackers will shut down our digital economy. Furthermore, the confidentiality, integrity and availability of sensitive data belonging to these organizations and government sectors in Nigeria are at great risk. Again, the theft of sensitive data from the government and military intelligence could bring a whole nation down. Therefore, the proposed digital forensics and cybersecurity approach is aimed at investigating, detecting, uncovering and interpreting any fraud associated with critical cyber infrastructures for the government and military. This will make the Nigerian digital ecosystem free of cyber attackers and strengthen

military intelligence. The proposed digital surveillance software can be of worth for
the following:

- Passive forensic investigations: Investigations where an attack has already
occurred.
- Active forensic investigations: Real-time investigations to track attackers at the
spot.

This is timely because, recently, the Nigerian military has depended so much on
sensors, networks, bandwidth and surveillance to perform their intelligent tasks.
Furthermore, industrial control systems such as supervisory and control data acquisition (SCADA) systems are vulnerable to different cyber attacks. These networks
and other cyber infrastructure usually contain very sensitive information. Terrorists
and other attackers usually target these cyber infrastructures for their dubious activities. However, proper forensic techniques/cybersecurity will fight even advanced
attackers. Economic crimes have risen around the globe as business and public sector organizations struggle in the face of economic austerity and spending cuts. Cyber
crimes are on a very high scale in Nigeria. For example, in June 2016, it was recorded
by the Punch newspaper that Nigeria is ranked 16th in the cyber attacks vulnerability index in Africa [7]. Furthermore, in March 2017, President Muhammadu Buhari
lamented that Nigeria losses N127 billion annually to cyber crime [8]. This is scary
and clearly shows that cyber crimes are on a rise in Nigeria. In view of these challenges, in 2014, the Nigerian government enacted the Cybercrime bill [9] to provide
for the prohibition, prevention, detection, response and prosecution of cyber crimes
in the nation. Recently, President Muhammadu Buhari signed the Nigerian Financial
Intelligence Unit (NFIU) Bill into law to handle financial fraud and related activities [10]. It is clear that the Nigerian government is doing her best to tackle these
crimes. However, to investigate, detect, uncover and interpret any fraud associated
with critical cyber infrastructures and to bring criminals to justice, the need to train
and equip e-crime fighters to successfully combat these crimes cannot be overem-
phasized. The financial and reputational risks of economic crime and disputes have
been on a large scale. The implementation of digital forensics and cybersecurity will
help prevent crimes locally and nationally and also secure our cyber infrastructure
for military intelligence. Taking action to assist in preventing terrorism, herdsmen
attacks, cyber crimes and other related crimes will save the government from huge
financial damage, reputational damage and protect the lives of its citizens. With the
high rate of crime in our society today, and the need to curb crime and ensure justice
for Nigerians, this research aims at ensuring fair trial of suspects by developing an
application that can be used by the National Intelligence Agency (NIA), the Criminal Investigation Department (CID) of the Nigerian Police, the Department of State
Security (DSS), State Security Service (SSS), the Nigerian Army, etc. to obtain digital evidence such as location, call log, SMS, contacts, from a suspect's smartphone
to aid criminal investigation and court proceedings.

This chapter is centred on the design of a software for retrieving digital evidence
such as location, call log, SMS, contacts, from mobile devices. This research work
entails the implementation and demonstration of the software, aimed at aiding the

criminal investigation department in solving crimes and also for court proceedings. This research is carried out for the criminal investigation department and any other agencies for fighting crimes in Nigeria as such, it won't be available to the general public. The objectives of this chapter are to develop a software that

1. Properly investigates and assists in the prosecution of cases involving digital evidence.
2. Preserves the integrity of seized digital evidence.
3. Provides expert testimony in court.
4. Acts as an educational and training resource for the criminal investigation department.
5. Enhances the capabilities of Nigerian law enforcement agencies in the investigation and prosecution of crimes that involve the use of computers, tablets, cellular phones.

5.2 System Analysis and Design

In any research, it is essential to carry out a system study or system survey of what is obtainable in the present system. This involves obtaining an adequate understanding of the present system processes, procedures and the basic problem areas of the present system in order to determine precisely what must be accomplished and how to accomplish it. This will enable the researcher to have a very good understanding of the working system. The methodology adopted for this research work is the structured system analysis and design methodology (SSADM). It has three levels namely:

1. The Data View: This describes all of the data and information the system (A-BOT) uses.
2. The Process View: This is a description of all the processes or actions performed by the system.
3. The Event View: These are the triggers that set all the processes in the system running.

Based on these different views, it gives the designer/developer of the system more information about the entire system (A-BOT) under consideration. It is worth noting that the SSADM is used by different departments in the United Kingdom government and even in non- governmental contractors. This is to achieve disciplined engineering approach and improve the quality of the entire system that is developed [11].

5.3 Product Features and How It Works

The A-BOT has the following valuable features namely:

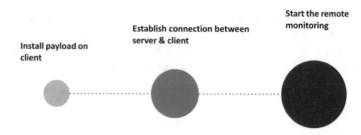

Install payload on client

Establish connection between server & client

Start the remote monitoring

Fig. 5.1 Digital surveillance software (A-BOT)

1. Client: This is usually installed on the attacker's digital device (phone or computer).
2. Server: This is installed on the investigator's system.
3. Payload: The payload is remotely sent to the attacker.

These features aid the forensic investigator to remotely get the attackers location, short message service (SMS) call logs and contacts on the digital device. Figure 5.1 shows how the A-BOT works.

The system (A-BOT) works by remotely installing the payload on the client system without his/her knowledge. Furthermore, the server is installed on the forensic expert/investigators system. Once both systems are online and a connection is established, the remote monitoring starts. The monitoring is done actively or passively. It is done actively when a forensic expert sits on his/her server and monitors exactly what the attacker is doing instantly. It is done passively when a forensic expert logs onto his/her server later to refresh and go through all the activities the attacker has done over a period of time. It is worth noting that Nigeria is spending so much on security but it is unfortunate that the rate of crimes is increasing. For example, Nigeria spent 1.334 trillion Naira for security in 2018 [12]. This amount will keep increasing if this security challenge is not properly addressed. This assertion could be true based on the fact that previous years had lower security budgets as compared to 2018 as shown in Fig. 5.2.

The damage is not only in terms of money but also in lives. For example, 5,113 persons from January 2018 to November 2018 were killed by insecurity issues ranging from Boko Haram attacks, herdsmen attacks, cult clashes and armed robbery among other several other reasons as shown in Fig. 5.3.

Hence, this proposed system (A-BOT) is very valuable for digital surveillance of the Nigerian cyber space either in for active forensic or passive forensic investigations.

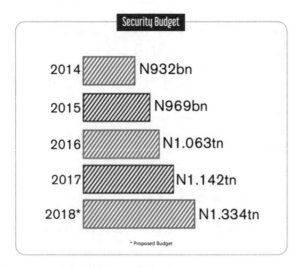

Fig. 5.2 Nigeria security budget from 2014–2018 [12]

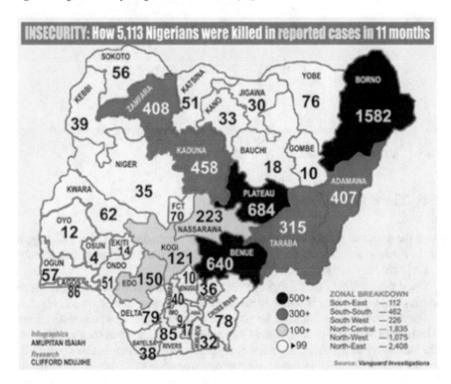

Fig. 5.3 Death due to insecurity of Nigeria in 11 months [13]

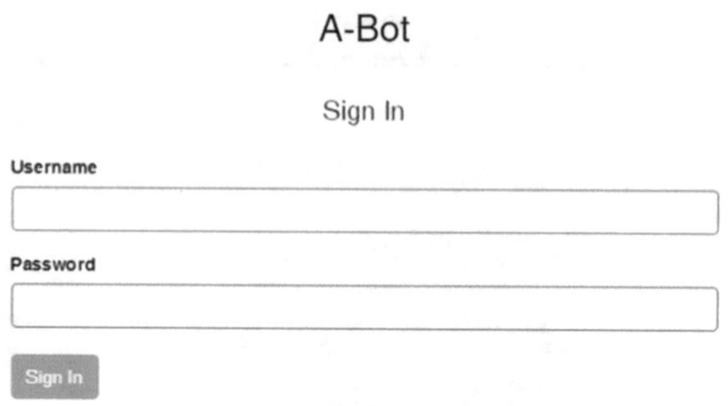

A-Bot

Sign In

Username

Password

Sign In

Fig. 5.4 A-BOT Login

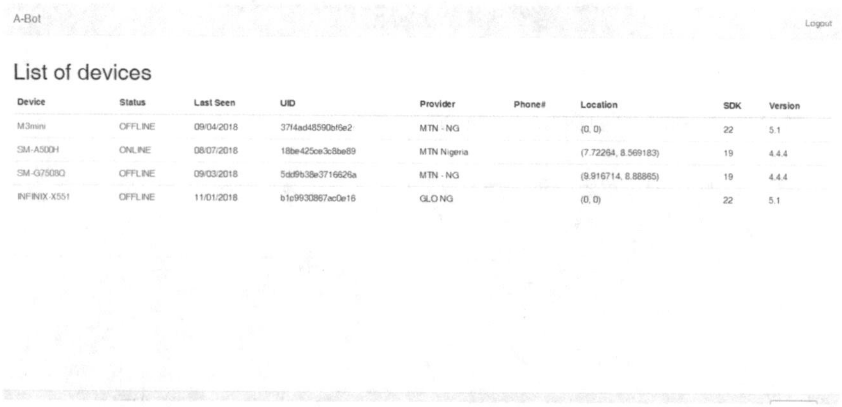

A-Bot   Logout

List of devices

Device	Status	Last Seen	UID	Provider	Phone#	Location	SDK	Version
M3mini	OFFLINE	09/04/2018	3714ad48590bf6e2	MTN - NG		(0, 0)	22	5.1
SM-A500H	ONLINE	08/07/2018	18be425ce3c8be89	MTN Nigeria		(7.72264, 8.569183)	19	4.4.4
SM-G7508Q	OFFLINE	09/03/2018	5dd9b38e3716626a	MTN - NG		(9.916714, 8.88865)	19	4.4.4
INFINIX-X551	OFFLINE	11/01/2018	b1c9930867ac0e16	GLO NG		(0, 0)	22	5.1

Fig. 5.5 A-BOT List of Devices

5.4 The Solution (A-BOT)

First, the designed system has a secured login page as shown in Fig. 5.4. This page is for the investigator. As such, the user name and password will be changed periodically to avoid attacks from hackers.

Once the forensic experts login to the digital surveillance software, the list of devices that the payload is remotely installed on are displayed as shown in Fig. 5.5.

Furthermore, the device to be investigated is opened for forensic investigations. When such a device is opened, it shows the location of an attacker as shown in Fig. 5.6. The location of an attacker has been very helpful in solving forensic cases especially when it relates to homicide, last location an attacker made a call, etc. As such, the A-BOT with the capability of showing the location of an attacker could assist in solving homicide, terrorism and related crimes. This will assist law enforcement agencies to track down an offender based on the location information provided by the A-BOT.

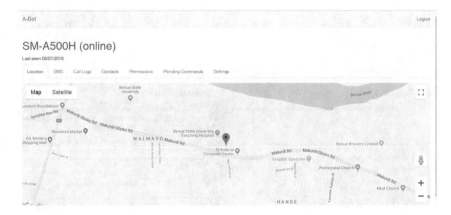

Fig. 5.6 A-BOT Location Detector

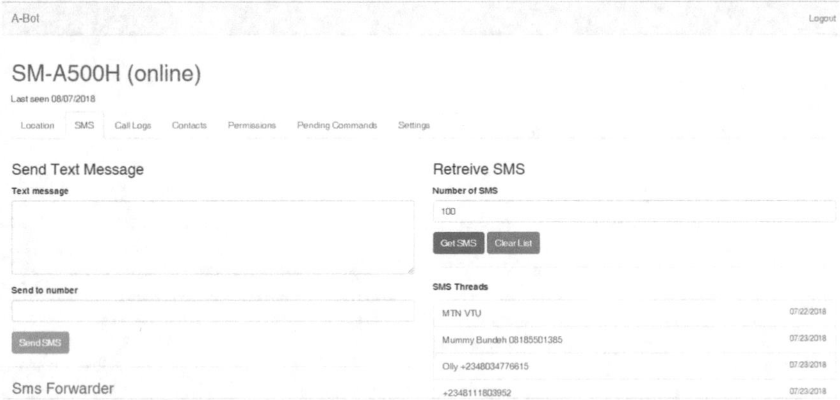

Fig. 5.7 A-BOT SMS

An important feature of the A-BOT is the capability it has in revealing the SMS of the attacker as shown in Fig. 5.7. Accessing the SMS of an attacker could be a rich form of evidence. This is because most people send SMS to their partners and as such, an investigation into an attackers SMSs could give an investigator a clear information about what actually occurred at the pre-attack.

The A-BOT also has the capability to show the call logs and contacts on an attackers device as shown in Figs. 5.8 and 5.9, respectively. These call logs and phone contacts could serve as a linkage between the real attacker (target) and the other people he/she transacts business with. This link could assist investigators in getting more attackers through who the attacker called and who called the attacker under investigation.

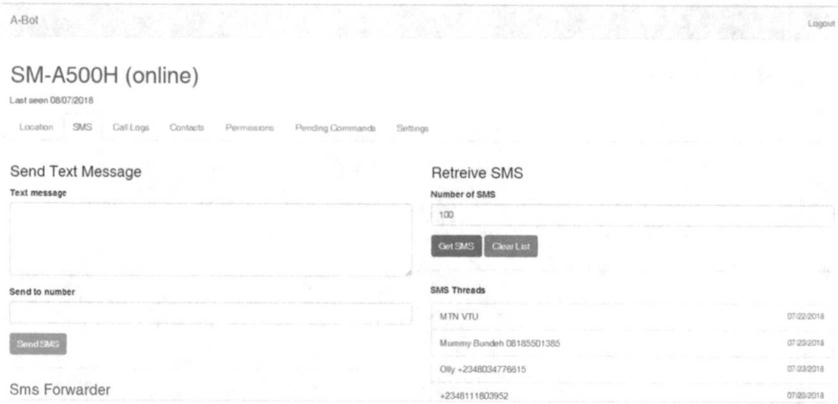

Fig. 5.8 A-BOT Call Logs

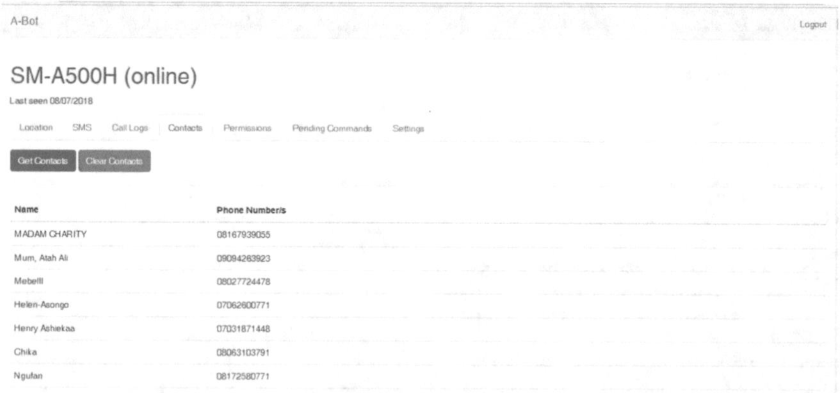

Fig. 5.9 A-BOT Contacts

5.5 Advantages of the Proposed System

The A-BOT has the following unique advantages:

1. Remote Installation: The A-BOT can be remotely installed on an attacker's digital device without his/her knowledge. This makes it a very fantastic tool for forensic experts.
2. An Indigenous Software: The A-BOT is developed in Nigeria and well tailored for tackling cyber and digital criminals in Nigeria.
3. Data Security: The system (A-BOT) has a secured login interface provided for the forensic expert to prevent unauthorized persons from accessing the system.
4. Digital Evidence for the Court: The captured evidence by the A-BOT is meant to be presented to the court of law to either acquit or convict a person under investigation.

5.6   Conclusion

The proposed solution (A-BOT) will secure critical cyber infrastructure and lives in Nigeria. The proper usage of this proposed system will serve as a digital surveillance and also prevent digital crimes in Nigeria. Furthermore, it will educate/train forensic experts capable of performing forensic investigations to make the Nigerian digital ecosystem free of cyber attackers. The A-BOT usage in Nigeria will follow the evidence extraction approach as described in Sect. 4.4.

Acknowledgements   The author would like to specially thank Agela Ebute and Emmanuel Okube for their assistance.

References

1. Smith J, Tran K (2017) Smartphone adoption on the upswing in Nigeria. https://www.businessinsider.com/smartphone-adoption-on-the-upswing-in-nigeria-2017-4?IR=T. Accessed 14 Jan 2019
2. Oserogho & Associates (2012). Legal Alert May 2012 Admissibility of Electronic Evidence. http://www.oseroghoassociates.com/articles/30-admissibility-of-electronic-evidence?print=1&download=0. Accessed 14 Jan 2019
3. Omolaye-Ajileye HJ (2016) Admissibility of electronic evidence in civil and criminal
4. Lessard J, Kessler GC (2010) Android forensics: simplifying cell phone examinations
5. Indiana University (2018). What is cyberinfrastructure? https://kb.iu.edu/d/auhf
6. Insidearewa (2018) Data is the oil of the digital Economy-DG NITDA. http://insidearewa.com.ng/2018/06/28/data-is-the-oil-of-the-digital-economy-dg-nitda/
7. Punch (2016) Nigeria ranks 16th in cyberattacks vulnerability index. http://punchng.com/nigeria-ranks-16th-cyberattacks-vulnerability-index/
8. Daily Post (2017) Nigeria losses N127b annually to Cyber Crime Buhari. http://dailypost.ng/2017/03/08/nigeria-losses-n127b-annually-cyber-crime-buhari%E2%80%8E/
9. Total Entrepreneurs (2014). Nigeria Senate Pass Cyber Crime Bill into Law with Penalty (Update on Recent Bills Passed in Record Time). http://thetotalentrepreneurs.com/nigeria-cyber-crime-bill/
10. Punch (2018). Buhari signs NFIU Act, separates unit from EFCC. http://punchng.com/buhari-signs-nfiu-act-separates-unit-from-efcc/
11. SSADM Views (2007). Outcome 1: Compare and Evaluate the Strengths and Weaknesses of Systems Development Methodologies. https://www.sqa.org.uk/e-learning/SDM01CD/page_04.htm
12. Yourbudgit (2018). 2018 Proposed Security Budget. http://yourbudgit.com/wp-content/uploads/2018/06/SECURITY-PROPOSED-2018-BUDGET.pdf
13. vanguardngr.com. How 5,113 Nigerians were killed in 11 months. https://www.vanguardngr.com/2019/01/how-5113-nigerians-were-killed-in-11-months/. Accessed 17 Jan 2019

Printed in the United States
By Bookmasters